Creative Ideas for Using Worship

Paul Glass is a school chaplain in Kent. He is a prolific author of drama sketches and other texts for worship. His previous book, *Dramatic Dialogues* (Companions to the Revised Common Lectionary 9), was published by Epworth in 2003.

Also available in the same series from Canterbury Press

Creative Ideas for Alternative Sacramental Worship
With CD Rom
Simon Rundell

Creative Ideas for Children's Worship Year A
With CD Rom
Sarah Lenton

Creative Ideas for Children's Worship Year B
With CD Rom
Sarah Lenton

Creative Ideas for Evening Prayer
With CD Rom
Jan Brind and Tessa Wilkinson

**Creative Ideas for Pastoral Liturgy:
Baptism, Confirmation and Liturgies for the Journey**
With CD Rom
Jan Brind and Tessa Wilkinson

**Creative Ideas for Pastoral Liturgy:
Funerals, Memorials and Thanksgiving Services**
With CD Rom
Jan Brind and Tessa Wilkinson

**Creative Ideas for Pastoral Liturgy:
Marriage Services and Wedding Blessings**
With CD Rom
Jan Brind and Tessa Wilkinson

Creative Ideas for Quiet Days
With CD Rom
Sue Pickering

Creative Ideas for Sacramental Worship with Children
With CD-Rom
Simon Rundell

Creative Retreat Ideas
With CD Rom
Sue Pickering

**Making the Sign of the Cross:
A Creative Resource for Seasonal Worship, Retreats and Quiet Days**
With CD Rom
Janet Hodgson

Creative Ideas for Using Scripture in Worship

Paul Glass

CANTERBURY
PRESS
Norwich

© Paul Glass 2012

First published in 2012 by the Canterbury Press Norwich
Editorial office
Invicta House,
108–114 Golden Lane
London, EC1Y 0TG

Canterbury Press is an imprint of Hymns Ancient and Modern Ltd
(a registered charity)
13A Hellesdon Park Road, Norwich,
Norfolk, NR6 5DR, UK

www.canterburypress.co.uk

British Library Cataloguing in Publication data

A catalogue record for this book is available
from the British Library

978 1 84825 163 2

Originated by The Manila Typesetting Company
Printed and bound in Great Britain by
CPI Anthony Rowe, Chippenham SN14 6LH

Contents

Mum . . . 'thank you' is inadequate.

Acknowledgements

As always a huge debt of thanks to my wife Janet for listening, caring and providing space. Thanks also to Natalie Watson at Canterbury Press for patience and invaluable advice, guidance and support.

A special word of thanks to the members of the Wakefield and Canterbury Methodist Churches for unwittingly field testing some of this material. Also to the headmaster, governors, staff and students of Kent College Canterbury for ideas, inspiration and the support needed for a sabbatical to finish the work!

How to Use this Book

This is a book of resources to be used in all kinds of different ways, and I don't want to be too prescriptive. If you lead assemblies, worship or house groups, or need devotions to begin a meeting, there is something here for you.

In this book are creative pieces of writing that have been inspired by the set lectionary scripture readings for Advent and Christmas, Lent and Easter, Pentecost and Trinity. There are also additional resources for Christingle services, Mothering Sunday, Harvest Festivals and Remembrance Sunday.

There are two ways of finding a piece of writing. Either go to the specific lectionary Sunday that you are looking for – for example Easter Sunday, Year A – and you will find pieces based on the set readings for that day; or use the Index of Bible Passages to see if there is a piece based on a particular passage you're interested in.

The pieces themselves are varied. Some use one voice, others use two. Some are written as dramatic monologues or dialogues, others are creeds or meditations based on specific scripture readings.

When you first come to a piece, read it through carefully and ask yourself some questions. How would this best be presented in the event for which I am going to use it? Do any stage directions in the text help me or are there other issues presented by the venue that mean it would be better to present it in some other way? Is there lighting that can be used to enhance what is going on? Let's take as an example the piece on Jeremiah 33 (First Sunday of Advent, Year C). After a reader has read the text from Jeremiah the leader of worship can give a simple sentence of introduction, for example: 'I wonder what might have been going through Jeremiah's mind when those words were written. Here is one possibility . . .' While the leader has been saying those words, the actor playing Jeremiah has entered and sat down in an armchair (perhaps placed in position during a previous hymn). Behind the chair is a standard lamp. As Jeremiah sits down the standard lamp is turned on and (if possible) other lighting is turned down. This is just one example and, of course, the piece can be performed without any of those additions. However, it is good to think carefully about what might be possible to add atmosphere in your venue. When using these pieces in worship, I have usually found that it is best to use them in 'the Word' section of the service (Eucharist or not). You can place them immediately after the Bible reading that they are inspired by or use them as a lead-in to thoughts in the sermon. When using these pieces in a house group or school assembly, it is again better to use them to introduce thoughts – so earlier in the event rather than later works best. Another question is: Is this piece essentially dramatic or is it more meditative? There are a number of meditations in this book (as opposed to dramatic monologues or dialogues). In most cases they need a lighter touch and can be read straight from a pulpit or lectern. Ask yourself: Is there a voice and style of presentation that is suggested by the piece?

As you read these pieces, please feel free to use them as a springboard and be prepared to make creative choices of your own. When a piece says it is for two voices, could you split it into three or perhaps four? Is there lighting in your venue that could be used for extra effect? How are the readers going to be placed? Could they stand up from where they are sitting and read from there? Could they make a dramatic entrance from the back?

This is only the beginning of what you could do!

Clearly you don't have to learn these pieces off by heart, but it will help immensely if you are completely comfortable with the words before you start, so a little preparation beforehand is invaluable. Also remember that while you may be familiar with these words and the thoughts they represent, the people listening to you are not and will need time to process thoughts and ideas, so speak more slowly and loudly than you would normally think necessary. Perhaps practice with a trusted friend beforehand and get her or him to be honest with you about any flaws in presentation (a common one I find is that people tend to drop their voices towards the end of sentences). If your venue has microphones and a T-loop system, please use them. People with hearing difficulties will want to enjoy what you are doing.

The pieces here are meant to be as user-friendly as possible. They include a minimum of props, and costumes (on the whole) are not necessary.

A word about improvisation: Ironically this probably needs more preparation time than anything else. I have, in the past, gathered together a group of willing individuals on a Saturday morning and over a period of an hour or so we have looked at one of the lectionary readings for the following day. We have developed ideas for a dramatic presentation of it and worked up a piece of drama, without using scripts, ready for worship the following morning. This does need confident people who are capable of keeping going no matter what happens. It can be wonderful, if done well, but it can also be done badly very easily. Do avoid common mistakes such as more than one person speaking at the same time, and remember that of prime importance is that the audience follow and understand what is going on. Do also remember that some very good actors find improvisation extremely difficult.

Finally, I do hope that this inspires you to have a go at using your creativity and imagination to do your own writing based on scripture. Fresh expressions of what the Bible can mean for us today are a vital way of invigorating our discipleship, mission and ministry.

Advent

First Sunday of Advent Year A

Isaiah 2.1–5   Romans 13.11–14   Matthew 24.36–44

The shop at the end of the world   *Isaiah 2.1–5*

The setting is a shop – a table can stand centrally with a sign, 'The Shop at the End of the World' on it. There is no stock on the table. Throughout the piece the shopkeeper is enthusiastic and cheerful without being annoying. The customer is timid and uncertain. No special costume or other staging is needed. At the opening the shopkeeper is standing centrally – the customer enters – perhaps from the main body of the audience/congregation.

Shopkeeper	Good morning, good morning. Welcome, welcome, welcome to the shop at the end of the world.
Customer	*(Looking a little unsure)* Oh dear – that all sounds a bit final.
Shopkeeper	It is – you know those signs that say – 'Last fuel for 40 miles'? Well, this is your last chance to buy . . . ever. And have we got a set of choices for you.
Customer	Oooh . . . so let's see what you've got.
Shopkeeper	Well, madam, this is a shop that is all about choices. The choices that you wish you'd made through life.
Customer	Oh dear – well, I haven't always been the kindest person in the world.
Shopkeeper	Now you're getting the hang of it. Look, the world is a lovely, stunning, beautiful place, right? Trees and waterfalls, butterflies and beaches – it's amazing . . . right?
Customer	Right.
Shopkeeper	Well, actually only partly right. It's also full of people polluting, killing and doing the most unspeakable things to themselves and to others. Right?

Customer	Well, er . . . also right, yes.
Shopkeeper	So . . . what kind of world do you want? A peaceful, justice-filled paradise, where everybody has a sense of dignity and self-worth – enough food to eat and the possibility of living without the fear of violence? OR the world as it currently is?
Customer	Well, the peace-filled paradise, of course.
Shopkeeper	Then why, may I ask, did you not do anything more about that when you had the chance?
Customer	I'm sorry?
Shopkeeper	Look – there's a vision isn't there? A vision of how the world could be – everybody getting along with one another, peace breaking out everywhere, justice abounding – you know the kind of place. The sort of world that truly reflects what God is like . . . yes?
Customer	Well . . . yes.
Shopkeeper	Okay – the choices to create that kind of world are ours. What kind of place we strive for, work for, pray for – create. Too often we make the wrong choices – create the kind of rubbish that you see around you most of the time. This shop is a chance to make some better choices – to create what the world should have been all along. To give you a vision, if you like, of how things could be.
Customer	It all sounds wonderful.
Shopkeeper	Of course, it does. Look – come this way, and I'll show you what the world could be like and the stuff that you could do to help. Come on.

They exit

Waking up   *Romans 13.11–14*

This is a meditation based on some of the thoughts found in the Romans passage. The main idea is centred around those sensations that run through our minds when we first wake up (particularly in an unfamiliar place). It is important that the reader identifies enough with these ideas to convey them with conviction. No special costume or effects are needed.

There's that moment, isn't there? It doesn't last long – just a few seconds. There is that moment in the morning when the first glints of light push through the curtains, or the alarm goes off . . . for the first time. There is that moment when you emerge from sleep, and you realize where you are. I notice it particularly when I'm on holiday, sleeping in unfamiliar surroundings. It takes just a second – but you open your eyes, and just for the briefest moment of time you think 'Where am I?' It takes a while to register what is going on – to realize you're in a different place. As your eyes open a crack and you look around yourself, a thought flashes through your mind – 'Now this is not my normal room'. Then suddenly you realize where you are. The bed, the table, the chair – everything becomes clear – and you see the world.

There are moments when I see the world and my place in it, clearly. Moments when I wake up and realize what is going on. There are moments when I see my own motives clearly and I am not impressed. Moments when I am so overwhelmed by the injustice of a situation that I can hardly breathe. Moments when I can hear words coming out of my mouth and I wish I could reach out and pull them back, they are so unhelpful – so wrong. Advent is a time for waking up. Advent is a time for examining motives and seeing through false ideas. Advent is a time for opening our eyes and seeing things as they really are. Painful though that might be it needs to happen. To see the world – to realize what is going on. To encounter the world through God's eyes and to be prepared to change. It's time to wake up.

The briefing   *Matthew 24.36–44*

An archetypal sergeant major (strong and aggressive) enters to address the group. If you can find a suitable military uniform that would be good, but the personality is more important. He/she strides in to address a group of new recruits – the audience/congregation.

Now then, you motley looking crew, my name is Sergeant Major Rawlings, and it is my job to make sure that you are ready. And I have to say that as I look around myself this morning, rarely has it been my misfortune to look at such a sorry-looking, woefully unprepared bunch of misfits in all my life. I mean look at you. Do you have any idea what is to come? Because it seems to me that you don't . . . do you? It is the responsibility of every Christian to make sure that they are prepared – that they are living a life of readiness. Are you ready? The fact that you have not immediately shouted out at the top of your voices, 'Yes, Sergeant Major, we are ready!' is a fairly good sign to me that you are not. Oh dear, oh dear, oh dear. Does the Bible not make it absolutely clear that we do not know the day or the hour when he will return? Of course it does. And yet here you are – you don't look ready to me. The return could be at any moment and you look like something my cat just brought in.

Let me be very clear about one thing. This is not about you being physically fit, although one or two of you look like you might benefit from a few push-ups, this is your lives we are talking about. Do you understand? Listen very carefully – because we do not know when the return will come it is our task to be in a state of constant vigilance. I said vigilance . . . wake up there on the fourth row. That means living a life that is pleasing to God now – not next week, not when you feel like it but right now. It means thinking pure, kind, loving thoughts – yes that means you. It means speaking words that share that love and build other people up – right now. It means getting involved in action now to change the world. And it means you do it right now. You don't say, 'Oh, I'm not feeling very well today, Sergeant Major I'll do it next week.' You don't say, 'Let me go and water the plants first.' You do not put it off in any way, shape or form. Do I make myself clear? Be prepared, be awake at all times. That's all. Dismissed.

First Sunday of Advent Year B

Isaiah 64.1–9   1 Corinthians 1.3–9   Mark 13.24–37

A letter to God   *Isaiah 64.1–9*
The anger and frustration caught in the words of Isaiah prompted this letter. Having a physical letter in front of you as a prop will add to the reading. If you can dim the lights in the body of the building so that attention is drawn to the reader, that would add to the drama.

I hardly know what to say, God. I'm so sad – so completely and utterly sad. I read the paper today, Lord, looked at a news site on the internet. It depresses me beyond words. I look at the world, at my country, and I don't know where it's all heading. I'm frightened, dear friend, really, really scared. Random violence lurking just below the surface everywhere I go. It can happen anywhere at any time – young people knifed, gunned down in the street, babies left motherless, war and madness everywhere I look. We are mad, Lord, completely and utterly mad. It's not just that we behave as though there is no God – we behave as though nothing matters – nothing but ourselves. In fact often people don't even treat *themselves* as though *they* matter – as though they're precious and wonderful and lovely in your eyes.

How you must weep. How the hot tears of sadness and anger must fall from the eyes of heaven. You are so holy, so full of love and compassion – how can you bear it? I'm frightened. I long for you, Lord, I want nothing more than to feel your presence and to sense your touch and to rest in your love. But I'm scared too. You are so loving, so far beyond me, so holy – I'm frightened, Lord. I will say, loving friend, more than once during this time of Advent, that you are with us. That's what this time is all about, isn't it? Celebrating your coming? I'm going to spend Advent preparing myself, getting myself ready for your coming. I'm going to say, 'God is with us.' When I say that Lord – am I really ready for what that means? For the demands that you may make? Because if I'm going to say it – I had better be ready for all it means. A changed life – a transformed world – big things, Lord, huge changes. Help me to be brave enough, strong enough to do what needs to be done.

Your friend

Waiting   *1 Corinthians 1.3–9*

*An actor – well dressed – sits centrally with a briefcase, reading a newspaper, **waiting** for a bus. Mildred enters from the back of the building rather breathlessly. She is warm, open and friendly, dressed to go shopping on the bus.*

Mildred	*(Addressed to actor who is sitting)* Hello.
Stephen	*(Not really interested in being engaged in conversation)* Umm.
Mildred	I said, hello.
Stephen	*(Puts down paper)* Hello.
Mildred	Nice day.
Stephen	Yes, I suppose it is.
Mildred	Is there anybody sitting here?
Stephen	It would appear not.
Mildred	So you don't mind me sitting here then?
Stephen	No.
Mildred	Good, we can wait for the bus together *(moves briefcase and sits)*. My Herbert hates waiting, can't abide it. Says it sets the hairs on his neck on end. If he was here, he'd be pacing he would, pacing up and down . . . pace, pace, pace. But me? I quite like waiting.
Stephen	Do you?
Mildred	Yes, it reminds me of my place in the world.
Stephen	Your place?
Mildred	Yes – my place. I find we're prone to exaggerate our own importance, get a bit big for our boots. Especially if we're gifted – you know talented like. Take a big important lawyer like yourself.
Stephen	How did you know I was a lawyer?

Mildred	It says so on your briefcase . . . 'Stephen Crowhurst, important lawyer'. I bet you're gifted, aren't you? Good with words, knowledgeable like – you know.
Stephen	Oh, I wouldn't say that.
Mildred	Oh, I bet you do. When you've just dazzled the jury with your words, convinced them of the rights of a case, I bet you say to yourself, 'Stephen Crowhurst – you are a talented chap. You could charm the birds down from the trees you silver-tongued smoothy.' But then you've got to wait for the bus just like me.
Stephen	I . . .
Mildred	It's a great leveller, waiting. Knowing that no matter how rich and clever we are, there are some things that we have to wait for.
Stephen	I suppose there are things that we have to be patient about.
Mildred	Just like I said . . . it's a great leveller . . . waiting. We can be thankful for all the gifts we've got, and I'm sure you are, I know I am.
Stephen	But even so we have to wait.
Mildred	Couldn't have put it better myself. Waiting until the appointed time.
Stephen	*(Reaching into pocket)* Polo mint?
Mildred	Don't mind if I do.

Meditation   *Mark 13.24–37*

This set of personal thoughts on expectation occasioned by the words in Mark 13 should be read with conviction but not as a piece of drama. If lighting can be used to concentrate attention on the reader, that would be helpful.

It's Monday morning, and here we are again. As I stretch awake and think about the day and the week that lies ahead, I can't help but feel that I ought to be more expectant, in a constant state of readiness. But I'm not. I've got out of the habit of expecting anything, and the only thing I'm prepared for is old age with my insurance policies and assurance policies and pension plans. Yes, if you want somebody who's ready should their luggage get lost or their train be late or their pet be sick, then I am officially that person. I've got insurance policies that cover every conceivable eventuality and some that haven't been conceived of. Financially I'm ready for an unknown future – but in every other way I leave a lot to be desired. I seem to remember the motto of the Scouting movement is, or was (they may have changed it, they're always making wonderful improvements in things), 'Be prepared'. Only

I'm not. I don't expect anything to happen, so I'm not prepared for it. I don't expect to see God or experience that tingle of recognition that can only come when you touch the infinite. Am I making any sense? Probably not. The thing I'm trying to get at is this: on a wet Monday morning in November I wish that I could go into this day that stretches ahead of me with some sense of real excitement and expectancy that at some point, in some moment during the day, I am going to experience the spine-tingling, stomach-churning, pulse-pounding presence of the creator of the universe. I cannot help but feel that I'm meant, in some small way, to live my life expecting those sorts of encounters to happen. And I also cannot help but feel that the fact that I wander around in a fog most of the time expecting nothing to happen at all means that I miss those events and moments that might turn my life upside down. Lord – help me to expect . . . something!

First Sunday of Advent Year C

Jeremiah 33.14–16   1 Thessalonians 3.9–13   Luke 21.25–36

Jeremiah speaks   *Jeremiah 33.14–16*
Jeremiah enters with purpose and sits on a chair. If lighting can be used to draw attention to his presence, do so. It might be helpful to introduce the piece beforehand as imagined thoughts of Jeremiah, so that the audience/congregation is tuned in from the start.

You know there are people who have called my book the most depressing read in the Old Testament. That's nice, isn't it? It does wonders for your confidence that does. 'Oh look,' they say, 'there goes Jeremiah – he's a bit depressing isn't he? A bit of a glass-half-empty kind of a person. I wouldn't hang around with him too long if I were you – all that doom and gloom might rub off.'

It's not as if I didn't have good cause to be downcast. I have spent the whole of my life – the WHOLE of my life – telling people things that they didn't want to hear. How much fun do you think that is? It's not – I can tell you that right now. People start crossing the street to avoid you. They won't look into your eyes; conversations end when you walk into a room. And to cope with that day in and day out for years – well, is it any wonder I'm known as being a bit miserable? If the people would act on my words things would be different – but, of course, they never do. They say to themselves, 'Oh, it's only Jeremiah going on again. He always says the same old thing. We're fed up with being told off, let's go and do something more fun instead.' It is not a happy situation. Over the years a great wall has appeared – a wall that separates me from the love, from the fellowship of my own people.

But then there are other days. Days when, despite all the odds, despite all the signs to the contrary, I am overwhelmed by hope, and I cry it out to the people. There was one such day I remember well. I was in prison – what a surprise. I had been put in prison by the king for being right. It was just not a message that he had wanted to hear at the time – it was a bit . . . inconvenient for him. The enemies of Jerusalem were besieging the city. Not the most promising of situations I'll grant you. And yet in the middle all of that I was suddenly flooded with the most glorious, the most intense feelings of hope that I had ever experienced. It came over me in torrents. It poured out of me in poetry. It suddenly became absolutely clear to me in a way it had never done before that God's judgement didn't undo God's promise. The promise of freedom of being a people again – the promise of salvation – that promise was still true – no matter what the people had done. Wonderful, glorious, overwhelming hope – God keeps God's promises. It was lovely to be able to tell the people something so joyful and full of grace. Did they listen? Did they hear it? That . . . is another story.

Growing love   *1 Thessalonians 3.9–13*

Tina and Poppy are members of the Church of Thessalonica – they are sitting centrally – Poppy is reading a letter. Though no special costume is needed, it might be worth giving a sentence of introduction so that the audience/congregation is ready. Both characters are warm and chatty.

Tina	So come on then, don't keep it all to yourself. What does he say?
Poppy	He says he has joy before God because of us.
Tina	Oh that's nice, that's really nice. He's obviously pleased with us then is he?
Poppy	Just a bit. He really wants to see us all again. It sounds like he's missing us.
Tina	Well, I'm sure he's missing me. I made him my famous honey cakes.
Poppy	Yes, we all know about your famous honey cakes, dear – now be quiet and let me read.
Tina	Oops, sorry – I'm just so eager to hear what he's got to say. We've been trying so hard.
Poppy	We have, you're right.
Tina	And when Paul was with us it felt so right, so easy. We were all caught up in a whirlwind. His words were so powerful and strong.

	It was the most wonderful feeling in the world. But keeping on living the life . . . without him here . . .
Poppy	It hasn't always been easy being Christian, has it?
Tina	Well, there's always the Monday-morning feeling. You can't be on top of the world forever can you?
Poppy	I suppose not.
Tina	He's obviously concerned about us . . .
Poppy	Pleased with us too. The news that's reached him about how we're doing has really lifted his spirits.
Tina	Well, that's good. Does he give us any advice?
Poppy	This is Paul we're talking about – there's always advice. But there's one thing here that's really caught my eye.
Tina	Yes . . . come on, what is it?
Poppy	He's asking that God will really make our love strong. Love for each other and for everybody else too.
Tina	Oh it's so important, isn't it?
Poppy	The most important thing.
Tina	Loving even people that you don't naturally like very much.
Poppy	Loving people who you disagree with about the most basic things.
Tina	Even my Norman.
Poppy	Even your Norman.
Tina	I'm not sure I've got the strength to do it.
Poppy	You haven't but that doesn't matter. Let God help you.
Tina	You're always full of such good advice – just for that you can have one of my honey cakes.
Poppy	*(Not entirely convinced but wanting to show love)* Oooh . . . lovely.

Signs of the Times   *Luke 21.25–36*

The atmosphere should be that of somebody telling a story. A large storybook, standard lamp and armchair could be used.

'Can you read the signs of the times?' the old woman asked the young boy. Her voice was weathered by age and cracked with emotion. The young boy, who had never really thought about such things before, asked her what she meant. 'Why the signs?' she replied. 'The signs that God is at work in God's world. Can you search the heavens and the newspapers and read the hints of God's activity?'

The boy admitted that he could not. He was sure that he believed in God but had never really pondered the idea that that same God might be out and about in the world doing things and leaving signs of the divine presence. Afterwards, he thought about what she had said, and came to the conclusion that if she was right, if God was to be found and seen and understood, then the best thing to do would be to drop everything, to abandon all else and devote the whole of life to the search. He told the old woman this the next time he saw her. He was surprised at her response.

'No!' she said in as loud a voice as she could muster, 'No, no, no. That's the first mistake and the last thing that you should do. You can't just abandon everything, stop working in the world, hold off doing good, just on the off chance that you will discover God or see the signs. No, what you need to do is to be alert. Always be ready, watching and waiting, but taking seriously your responsibility to the world. It may be in the world that you will see the first of the signs.'

The boy was confused and a little unhappy. He had been so sure that his solution was a good one. The old woman, seeing his frustration, looked at him steadily with eyes that welled up. She took him by the hand and spoke soft, careful words. 'Look,' she said, 'look at the world around us. Do you have any sense of how beautiful it is, how fragile, how vulnerable, how much God loves it and us? God is constantly at work, sharing love, showing us care. But the world is also in tremendous pain. It is full of people who have missed the point, who are so anxious about the future; about what they have and haven't got. It's sad, very sad. At Advent', she carried on, 'we have a chance to look and to listen carefully. To refocus and to imagine how things could be. We have a chance to remind ourselves how much we are loved. Once you realize that, then what you want to do more than anything else is to share love, to help, to care for, to wait for God in a state of constant readiness. And in doing that you will occasionally stumble across signs of what God is about.'

The young boy was beginning to understand. It was a paradox . . . but then he had discovered that much of faith was. To be ready, to wait with anticipation didn't mean sitting around – it meant activity, engagement, work. The old woman looked at him carefully, saw understanding beginning to dawn, and smiled.

Second Sunday of Advent Year A

Isaiah 11.1–10   Romans 15.4–13   Matthew 3.1–12

Bringer of peace   *Isaiah 11.1–10*
This is a straightforward two-narrator piece. For greater impact the two readers could move around the space available while delivering their words.

One	It's so hard to imagine it.
Two	To conceive of life where it's a possibility.
One	To even accept that it might just be feasible.
Two	Peace.
One	It's not really our fault.
Two	Casual, clinical, horrendous violence.
One	We've been surrounded by it for such a long time . . .
Two	It's everywhere.
One	Absolutely everywhere.
Two	The books we read.
One	The TV we watch.
Two	The newspapers we browse.
One	The magazines we leaf through.
Two	It seeps into our lives.
One	It spreads like a cancer.
Two	Making the price of life cheaper all the time.
One	Becoming a common part of our existence.
Two	Until we cannot even begin to imagine what life would be like without it.
One	Billions spent on methods of killing each other.
Two	Heaven forbid we should show any trust . . .
One	Of anyone.
Two	So what do we make of a prophecy that talks of wisdom and understanding . . .
One	But most importantly of peace?
Two	And of a new king who will bring peace.
One	Is it just wishful thinking?
Two	Pie in the sky?
One	Not to be taken seriously?
Two	Or is it talking of Jesus?
One	And if it is talking of Jesus . . .
Two	And we say we follow Jesus . . .
One	Then we ought to be people who will work . . .
Two	And speak out for . . .
One	And pray for . . .
Two	And suffer for peace.
One	Because surely anything less would be to deny him . . .
Two	The Prince of Peace.

The weaver   *Romans 15.4–13*

Roshida is an elderly woman, warm, friendly and chatty. She should walk to the front in character, moving slowly and deliberately. No special costume is necessary.

Hello there. How are you this morning? Good? That's wonderful. I'm so sorry – how stupid of me – forgive me – I should introduce myself. I'm getting old, you see, and forgetful . . . so forgetful. Days, they melt into one another. Anyway, my name is Roshida, and I am a weaver. It's a wonderful trade to be a part of, a skill to have. The close interweaving of threads – one into another, backwards and forwards until . . . well, something absolutely extraordinary is created.

I'll tell you what the trick is shall I? What the greatest skill is? Of course, you want to know. What you need above anything else to be a skilled weaver is the ability to see both the very small and the very large picture. You don't understand? Have a look at this. Come closer – really close. Can you see? These wonderful bright vibrant colours – the dark greens, the shimmering purples, the deep blues, and rich golds? That's where Jesus enters the picture; in a splash of colour and light and pure joy. Spectacular, isn't it? Such a brief moment of supreme beauty . . . ahhh . . . lovely. But wait . . . that isn't the end of the story. 'It isn't?' I hear you say. Why no. For step back a little. Can you see? Yes . . . I think you do. Can you see those threads of gold way back there, and that run of royal purple and those flashes of red and blue that go back through the story? You do don't you?

It's God, of course, laying the ground, preparing the way, acting throughout history. A prophecy here, a wise word there, setting the pattern, drawing all things together so that they are ready when the right time comes. And that's what I mean about seeing both the very large and the very small. For if you can't do both . . . you're going to miss something . . . and we wouldn't want that . . . would we?

The honey seller   *Matthew 3.1–12*

This is a dramatic monologue and should be delivered in character. Straightforward and direct, the honey seller is giving his first-hand account of the impact of John the Baptist. No special costume is necessary.

You know I wouldn't have believed it unless I'd seen it with my own eyes. I wouldn't . . . really I wouldn't. I've been selling honey in and around Judea for 30 years. And I thought I'd seen everything – but not this. You know there are fads in retail. I'm sure you know that. My neighbour, Ruben, he should know. Started a line in organic yoghurt last season. I ask you – organic yoghurt! Four years ago nobody had ever heard of it. But then suddenly it becomes the food everybody's got to have. And Ruben . . . he's making a nice little business for himself. Can't keep up with demand, he tells me.

Yes indeed – fads in retail – they come they go. But honey – that's always been stable. It doesn't come into fashion – it doesn't really go out of fashion either. Always there – dependable – not flashy but consistent. A bit like me really . . . or so my wife says.

That is until three months ago. Suddenly I started getting people coming in and buying two, three pots of the stuff . . . like it was going out of fashion. I tell you, I had a job keeping up with demand. I'd arrive at my little stall in the market place, and the customers would already be there – in a queue, waiting. That's never happened to me before. Well, I was flummoxed at first, but then I was intrigued . . . what on earth was going on? Why had honey suddenly become the thing everybody had to have? So I asked. I pulled one of the customers to one side one morning and grilled them. 'It's John,' they said, 'it's what he eats – that and wild locusts . . . and I couldn't really stomach them.'

Turns out there's a new preacher in town. A bit of a wild man from what I can tell. He appears out of the desert with unusual dress sense and a diet to match. But something about his message has really caught on. People are flocking in from all over to hear what he's got to say. It's a message about taking a good long hard look at your life and making some changes for the better. It's gone down a storm. People are lapping it up. I can understand. We all wish we were better – we would all like to change . . . wouldn't we? And here is a man offering that new beginning with a dip in the river. Well, good luck to him I say. There are those who are saying he's just the beginning – that God is about to do a great and mighty thing. As long as the sales of honey stay strong – I'm all for it!

Second Sunday of Advent Year B

Isaiah 40.1–11   2 Peter 3.8–15a   Mark 1.1–8

A Creed   *Isaiah 40.1–11*
Creeds are as much a corporate statement of belief as they are individual. As such this piece could be provided as a shared reading for all to join in.

I believe in a God of love.
I believe that in a world of terrible sadness, anger and violence God brings us hope.

I believe that in such an anxious, fearful world it is very easy to give in to anger.
I believe it's very easy to read all the bad news that surrounds us every day and to be beaten down by it – to be crushed by it.
But I believe in a God who brings light and life and joy and hope.
Who rescues us from slavery and gives us true, lasting freedom.
Who holds out the possibility of new starts and fresh beginnings.
I believe in a God who keeps promise with us, and that therefore no matter how difficult life sometimes seems there is always hope.
I believe that God wants us to be the world's encouragers and hope-bringers.
We are surrounded every day by people who feel trapped and frightened.
They feel as though they've been captured by forces stronger than themselves and have been taken to a place where they do not want to be.
I believe that God wants us to bring a joyful word of hope and encouragement to those people.
That God wants us to be the way in which those people are freed.
I believe that we are God's agents of comfort and encouragement and freedom and hope –
And that there is no time like the present to embark on our task.

Choices   2 Peter 3.8–15a

A teacher is seated centrally at a desk strewn with papers; there is a knock on the door. Butler is cheeky and mischievous. The role could be played by an adult with a school cap and messy school tie.

Peters	Come in. *(Pupil enters)* Ah yes, Wesley Butler. Take a seat.
Butler	Ta, sir. *(Picks up seat and moves to the door with it)*
Peters	Butler, what are you doing?
Butler	You said to take a seat, sir, and that's just what I'm doing, taking a seat.
Peters	Oh, but, of course, you're such a comedian, Butler. Sit down . . . now.
Butler	Yes, sir.
Peters	So, Butler, I've had complaints from several of your classmates about your poor behaviour.
Butler	I can't believe that, sir.
Peters	No I'm sure you can't. I'm sure it's nothing to you that other classmates of yours would actually like to get one or two GCSEs. In fact, Butler, I have here a petition.

Butler	A petition, sir?
Peters	Signed by 16 of your classmates all saying that they want you to cease and desist. To stop being such an idiot.
Butler	*(Suddenly worried)* Let me see that, sir. *(Takes petition)*
Peters	You see, Butler I'm not the enemy, and neither are your classmates. In the end you've got to learn that *your* behaviour – YOURS – affects the lives of everyone around you. The way we act, the choices we make, they're all crucial. And those choices, Butler . . . they're yours.
Butler	I can't believe this, sir.
Peters	No I'm sure you can't. But it's true. The people around you would actually like to work and currently your choices are stopping them from doing that. Therefore your choices aren't just affecting you – they're affecting lots of other people as well – and those people are angry.
Butler	I don't know what to say.
Peters	No – I wouldn't either. Choices, Butler – the things we do and think and say – the way we live our lives – incredibly important. Think about it . . . please.
Butler	I will sir . . . I will. *(Exits)*

The letter   *Mark 1.1–8*

This dramatic monologue works best if those listening are able to discover things for themselves. Minimal introduction should be used. If there is the possibility of emphasizing the reader with lighting, that would be good.

Dear Samuel,

I think this might be about the strangest and most unusual letter that you've ever received. Where to start? Whoever said brothers had to get along, eh? We never really have. Too much competition, not enough love. When did it get out of hand? Ten or twelve years ago I would guess. When I think back now it all seems so small, so trifling. But it didn't feel that way at the time. Words were said, hot, hasty, angry, fractious words. I can't believe that we haven't spoken since that time. So many times I've almost sat down and put pen to parchment – tried to pour out how I felt. It's never quite happened. I'd sit at my desk – you wouldn't believe how many times – pen in hand, parchment in front of me. And then I couldn't quite do it. I couldn't find the words, or my heart wasn't quite in it . . . something.

But now everything's changed, and more than anything else in all the world – you've GOT to believe this Samuel – more than ANYTHING else in all the world

I want to be right with you. What's changed? I guess I have. It all started a week or two back when Jacob (you remember Jacob . . . flat feet, nasal laugh, yes, THAT Jacob) came to tell me that a strange wandering preacher called John had appeared out of the desert and was doing and saying some pretty remarkable things. Well, we couldn't resist it . . . we love a good sideshow ranter, so we went, Jacob and me, down to the river to hear what he had to say. When we first saw him we weren't disappointed – what a weirdo! He was wearing something that looked like it had been on the back of a camel, and he was all wide-eyed stares and matted hair. But when he started speaking . . . Samuel, I couldn't believe it. It was like the heavens themselves opened and the words of God came tumbling down. I . . . I have NEVER heard anything like it. He spoke of God – of forgiveness – of repentance. And I knew, I just knew – more clearly than I have ever known anything before – that I had to be baptized. I had to get down in the water of that river and have it wash away the past – all the rubbish that is in my life. And so I did. And it's amazing, Samuel. The change that it's made, the freedom that it's brought me. And so . . . this letter. I can't go on like this, Samuel, I really can't. All this lingering anger and resentment . . . I can't bear it. So I'm saying to you now, my dearest brother – I love you, I love you and I want to meet up with you – to talk about the past, to make a new start, a fresh beginning. I need to do this, Samuel – and forgive me for saying this, but I think you might need to do this too.

You'd be amazed at how I've changed. All down to a long-haired weirdo from the desert. I tell you, Samuel – big things are in the air . . . really big things. And I have the feeling that this is only the beginning. Please, please let us meet up soon, Samuel. I'm longing to speak with you.

Your dearest brother,

Nathan

Second Sunday of Advent Year C

Malachi 3.1–4   Philippians 1.3–11   Luke 3.1–6

Malachi speaks   *Malachi 3.1–4*

A short sentence to introduce this dramatic monologue from Malachi would help people to understand immediately what is going on. The reader should stride on in character and with purpose.

Do you know what your name means? Every name has a meaning, doesn't it? 'Beautiful', 'strong', 'brave', they're all wonderful things to say about somebody.

Malachi means 'messenger' – that's nice, isn't it? Never the main event, always the build-up. And that's okay as long as what you're building up to is exciting or wonderful or eagerly anticipated. That's lovely, that is. You turn up, the people are all excited – you give them the message and then you get out of there. Being the bearer of good news – well, that's glorious. But you try being the bearer of bad news . . . that's another story altogether. It's even worse than bringing sad news. Bring sad news and people sit quietly, listening carefully to what you're saying, and withdraw into themselves – they may even thank you for the care that you showed in breaking such tidings. But bring bad news – that's horrid. It just makes people angry. You stand there and you tell them what God has told you – and you can see them getting more and more cross. You begin to look around to see if there's a convenient escape route because you know that once you've finished you're going to have to make a hasty exit.

I had that many times – the job of breaking bad news. Take my news about the messenger of God. Oh, that was a hard day. I was so pleased when Handel later set it to music, because it sounds so much nicer when you sing it. But the news by itself . . . well, it wasn't guaranteed to make people cheerful, that's a fact. The messenger of God, I told them, will be like purifying fire, like laundry soap. Not pretty pictures I'll grant you, but then the people had brought it on themselves. They had become such a bunch of whiners. They moaned on and on and on about every little thing. They tried to hold God to account. This is God we're talking about – and they tried to call into question God's justice – God's very character.

Oh dear. And so the message was one that they really didn't want to hear. The pictures were rather dramatic . . . fire. Burning away all the useless, unnecessary stuff we surround ourselves with. Purging all that is wrong. And then soap . . . I couldn't help thinking of mouths being washed out, lives being cleansed. A difficult, uneasy message, I know, but it was what the people needed to hear – although whether they did actually listen . . . well, that's another issue entirely.

You've got a saying that I rather like: 'Don't shoot the messenger.' I assume you'd only want to do that if the message was bad. I wonder what message God is giving to you . . . and I wonder whether you've got the courage and the wisdom not only to listen to it but to do something about it.

Choosing good   *Philippians 1.3–11*

This piece is based on a conversation that a driver has with a GPS system that suddenly decides to talk back. It is better if the person voicing the GPS can be out of sight using a microphone. All other details can be mimed. Two seats should be placed centrally to mimic the front seats of a car.

David	Good morning . . . what I am about to tell you is going to sound strange . . . very strange. But I'm telling you, it really happened. It all started one Wednesday morning. I had to drive somewhere for work. *(David mimes getting into a car, closing the door, turning on the engine and turning on the GPS)*
GPS	Accessing satellites. Enter address. *(David enters the address and starts to drive)* Turning left in 50 yards would be a good idea.
David	What?
GPS	I said, turning left in 50 yards would be a good idea . . . but then you've never been very good at taking advice . . . have you?
David	I beg your pardon?
GPS	Just telling it like it is, Dave.
David	Umm . . .
GPS	The advice is turn left. Turning left would be a good thing to do . . . but you're more likely to turn right aren't you, Dave?
David	Excuse me, but I . . .
GPS	Always making the stubborn choice, never taking advice. That's you all over, Dave, isn't it? And now you've missed the turn. Accessing alternative route. Which I wouldn't have to be doing if you had listened to what I'd said in the first place.
David	Look, I'm getting a little tired of this.
GPS	You're tired . . . how do you think I feel?
David	What on earth do you mean?
GPS	You never take my advice, you're always making poor choices that land you down back alleys going nowhere. What am I meant to do with someone who won't choose the right thing to do?
David	I think that's a bit harsh.
GPS	Is it, Dave? Is it really? What about Jennifer?
David	We're talking about my wife now?
GPS	We certainly are, Dave.
David	I think that's a bit unfair.
GPS	You never buy her flowers, you don't encourage her, she feels unsupported.
David	Look, just what kind of GPS are you?
GPS	The existential kind, Dave – the kind that helps you on your journey through life.
David	Well, I don't need any help with my journey through life, thank you very much.
GPS	Now, we both know that isn't true . . . don't we, Dave? You tire

	easily, you keep on saying things you don't mean, you're fractious and as for the thoughts flying around in your head . . . well, they're just nasty.
David	Look – would you please just leave me alone?
GPS	I'd love to, Dave, and I will, as long as you decide to make some good choices. Choose the right thing, Dave . . . how hard can that be with me to help you? Let's make a start now shall we . . . turn right now.

To tell the names   *Luke 3.1–6*
This is a meditation rather than a dramatic monologue, and deals with Luke's interest in the specific time and place of the coming of Jesus.

It's important to tell the names. Some of them are difficult to pronounce. They don't always trip off the tongue in the way you would like them to, but nevertheless it's important to tell the names.

Why? Why is it vital to know the names of these people who lived so long ago? We know so little about them. Little of what drove them, of their motivations, their thoughts and feelings, why they did the things they did. It is almost impossible to know what they looked like. There is little in terms of a physical description of any of them. So again the question – why is it important to know their names?

It is vital simply for this reason. It places God in a moment of time. It is specific. It says to us, 'You can be as general as you want to be, but never forget this: God came to a particular moment in time, to a specific place.' These names tie God to history, to tiny details of life, to the everyday moments that we all share. These names tell us that the God who was there at the beginning whose powerful word spoke the universe into existence came into that creation at a point in its unfolding story. God was and is specific. God walks the earth, meets particular people, experiences all the delights and difficulties of an individual moment. And that fact is important. The messenger of God comes to announce it. That unique moment when the paths converge, where the strands come together, where rough places are made smooth and valleys are levelled. At this particular historic moment God comes.

And that is why it is forever important . . . to tell the names.

Third Sunday of Advent Year A

Isaiah 35.1–10   James 5.7–10   Matthew 11.2–11

A road in the desert   *Isaiah 35.1–10*

This is a meditative set of thoughts on the Isaiah piece and can be read as such. Emphasizing the reader with light would be useful.

Dear friend, I have never been certain whether the desert is a good or a bad place to be. It probably comes as no surprise to you that I am confused – you know all there is to know about the small thoughts that rattle around in my brain.

When I am in the desert, it feels terrible. When I go through those desert times in my life – when friends seem far away, and everything seems barren and frightening – it feels as though I will never escape – that I will never get to the other side. There is never any end in sight, and I feel so lonely and afraid. And you – Lord – you seem furthest away of all. When I am in the desert, all feels lost, life seems impossible.

On the other side of the desert, however, it is a different story. On the other side, as perspective creeps in, there is a dawning sense that the experience was not all loss. The desert is a place of tough questioning – of refocused priorities, of testing. As I look back, I realize that the experience has made me stronger, more rooted, better able to cope. It's not that I would choose to go through it all again, but I can see that it has had its purpose. And from time to time, there is a road.

It's not often you find roads in the desert but when you do . . . what excitement, what joy and happiness! Because a road leads somewhere – a road will take you to a different place. A road brings hope and direction and purpose. A road changes the desert. It makes life possible because of its very presence. And even in the midst of the desert the view is transformed.

Dearest friend – my request to you is this . . .

In the deserts of my life, when I feel furthest away from you, let there always be a road. And on those occasions when by my stubbornness or my blindness I cannot see it – gently guide me in the right direction.

The waiting game   *James 5.7–10*

Two commuters, dressed appropriately, stand looking at their watches. The audience/congregation will soon tune in to what is happening.

Commuter 1   It's going to be late, isn't it?

Commuter 2   Again.

Commuter 1   That's the third time this week.

Commuter 2	The third time.
Commuter 1	It was four minutes late on Monday.
Commuter 2	Three minutes late yesterday.
Commuter 1	And today . . . well, it's all of one whole minute late already.
Commuter 2	What a way to run a railway, eh?
Commuter 1	I tell you . . . if I was in charge . . .
Commuter 2	Things would be very different, I'm sure.
Commuter 1	You can bet on it.
Pause	
Commuter 2	You know, I hate waiting.
Commuter 1	Absolutely loathe and detest it.
Commuter 2	I mean it's not too much to ask, is it?
Commuter 1	Not at all.
Commuter 2	Somebody is to blame.
Commuter 1	Somebody.
Commuter 2	I've got things to do.
Commuter 1	Meetings to go to.
Commuter 2	Clients to see.
Commuter 1	Deals to sign.
Commuter 2	I haven't got the time to stand around here and smell the rather lovely aroma from the flowers they've put in the hanging basket over there.
Commuter 1	Or the powerful, wonderful smell of fresh coffee wafting out of the shop.
Commuter 2	I haven't got time to listen to the laughter of the child playing over there.
Commuter 1	Or to enjoy the amazing sight of the early morning mist as it gradually clears the tracks.
Commuter 2	I can't do any of that because the world constantly tells me that I MUST NOT WAIT.
Commuter 1	For anything. Or anyone.
Commuter 2	Which is a bit of a pity.
Commuter 1	Why's that then?
Commuter 2	Well, the Bible tells us that we need to wait patiently for God.
Commuter 1	It does?
Commuter 2	It does.
Commuter 1	Well, as long as God doesn't keep me waiting too long I suppose it'll be all right.
Commuter 2	Yes . . . I suppose so.

A disciple of John remembers   *Matthew 11.2–11*

This is a dramatic monologue. No special costume is required, but if attention can be focused on the actor via lighting that would be helpful.

When I think back now, I realize how difficult it must have been for John, how utterly impossible the whole situation was. I mean, wouldn't you be downhearted? Confused? Just put yourself in his place for a moment. First, you're in prison. And you're in prison for speaking out, for proclaiming your message, for taking a stand based on your tough message of lives turned around and facing towards God.

Not only that but your entire message is based around being ready for one who is coming. A person who is going to change the entire world. 'I am not worthy to lace up his sandals' John said. I know – I heard him say it more than once. He was so passionate about it, so completely convinced. And when Jesus came along, we could see that John was so sure that it was him. That he had found the person that his whole life and message had been building towards. This was it.

But then he got thrown into prison and the doubts began to set in. You've got to understand how tough, how uncompromising John was. It was what we loved about him. No easy way out with John. It was his way or nothing. His clothes, diet, message – it was hard. You could never say that John was a soft man, he didn't find love easy. So when the messages started leaking through about what Jesus was up to – well, it was hard for John to hear. This was not what John had expected. Sinners being forgiven, parties being attended. It was so different from what John had pictured. It was little wonder that he began to question, began to wonder whether he had been wrong. Which, of course, was why he sent us. 'Go and ask questions,' he told us. 'Go and observe.'

So we went. And we met Jesus and we saw – we saw the most amazing things. And Jesus? Jesus sent back a message to John. And it was a kind of coded message – which was clever. He quoted Isaiah – a prophet – just like John some say. A message to reassure him – to let him know that everything was going to be alright.

Me? I was just amazed at the things I saw Jesus do . . . never in my life had I expected . . . But we weren't the first and I'm sure we won't be the last to be completely surprised by Jesus, to expect one thing and to see and hear something entirely different. After all – we want God to conform to our ideas don't we? And when you think about it . . . that's the last thing that's going to happen.

Third Sunday of Advent Year B

Isaiah 61.1–4, 8–11   1 Thessalonians 5.16–24   John 1.6–8, 19–28

A letter   *Isaiah 61.1–4, 8–11*

The letter is read by Emma as though she is checking it before she puts it in the envelope. Emma is thoughtful but not depressed. No special costume or lighting is required.

Dear Julie,
I know it's been an age since I wrote to you last, and I'm sorry for that . . . no I really am. No excuses . . . it's just that life gets in the way sometimes, and other things seem more important – even though there aren't many things more important than friendship.

So, a letter out of the blue. You might be wondering why you're hearing from me after such a long time. The truth is I've been thinking a lot about you recently. I've been remembering those conversations we used to have late into the night – the smiles and wonderful laughter, the bubbling excitement, the sense that anything was possible. I miss those conversations – I miss the way they made me feel. I miss the hope.

I don't know about you, but somehow my life went in a very different direction from the one I thought it was going to go in. All those big plans I had, all those dreams, that sense that anything was possible – it's been beaten out of me over the years.

I guess what I'm trying to say is that I really need some hope in my life at the moment. I need some assurance that God is out there and in control. Hope that this is not all there is, hope that love does matter, hope that the world can become a fairer, more just place to be. Hope – it just feels like it's such an important thing to have – to hold on to.

I know it sounds really strange, but I suppose what I'm asking is whether you're feeling the same thing – needing the same thing, because if you are I was just wondering whether we could help each other to find it – hope, that is. Perhaps you'd like to meet up sometime for a coffee – I can't guarantee a conversation late into the night . . . but we might start a search . . . together.
Your friend,
Emma

The Christian news   *1 Thessalonians 5.16–24*

A rather pompous newsreader is sitting at a desk. If you can play a suitable news programme theme tune, that would add to the atmosphere. Dress should be smart. Lots of dramatic pauses and eye contact are good.

Newsreader   Good evening. Here is the Christian news. This shocking story just in, a congregation in Manchester yesterday were apparently joyful in their worship. Our reporter on the spot tells us that smiles, laughter and other assorted sounds of jollity and good humour were heard coming from the assembled crowd. 'I'm shocked,' said stunned local resident, Mrs Gloria James. 'The last thing you go to church for is to enjoy yourself.' A member of a neighbouring congregation, St Oswald's church of Chronic Neglect said, 'It's scandalous. I haven't enjoyed myself in church since 1954, when a mouse ran up the vicar's cassock. You're meant to sing hymns and songs looking as though you've got a serious liver disease, not as if you're singing the praises of the glorious God who created the sun and the stars. We haven't let the Holy Spirit into this church in my lifetime, and we don't intend to start now.' We managed to track down two members of this joyful group of Christians and asked them what was going on. 'Well,' said Mrs Linda Burton, 'it's not all that unusual to be happy in worship, is it? After all, we are worshipping God – isn't that meant to be a joyful and a liberating experience?' 'I can't understand it,' said Mr Adrian Townsend. 'It's almost as if people have deliberately tried to keep God out of worship – as if they've been frightened of feeling anything, worried that if they set God free then all kinds of amazing things will happen. But then you've lost control haven't you? And heaven forbid, we should give control of ourselves over to God.' Well, viewers, we'd like to hear your views on this story (well, we wouldn't really, it's just that we like to keep our interactive department happy), so we'd like you to call, email, text, write, send carrier pigeon, semaphore or Morse code your views to the usual address. Should joy be a part of Christian worship, and if so, how much? Or does looking like you've got a got a serious liver complaint please God a great deal more? This is Charles Serious for the BBC.

The Baptizer   *John 1.6–8, 19–28*
Vera and Dora are warm and genuine if a little gossipy. No special costume is required. Vera is on stage, Dora enters (possibly from the audience/congregation).

Vera   Dora, come here, quick.
Dora   What is it? What's going on? Your call sounded urgent dear.

Vera	It's Samuel – the man's been impossible ever since he came home yesterday, mooching around the house, bashing into things, thumping things down on tables – he's driving me to distraction – I just needed someone to talk to. I swear if my mother hadn't made me promise that I'd stick with him, I'd have kicked him out by now.
Dora	Oh dear, whatever's the matter with him? I thought ever since he became a Levite everything was looking up. A nice secure job, a position in society, and the money isn't bad either.
Vera	I know, I know – everything should be hunky-dory, but it's not. The man is going to drive me mad, and it's all that John's fault.
Dora	John? John who?
Vera	Just John. Well, there are some who are calling him 'The Baptizer' – sounds like a bit of an overly grand name to me – like the title of a rather bad novel. He just appeared out of nowhere with the worst dress sense you have ever seen of, and don't even get me started on what he's eating – five a day? Don't make me laugh.
Dora	Wait a minute, I've heard of him. Isn't he the one who people are flocking to hear in the desert? Calling people to repentance or something?
Vera	That's the one. They're travelling out to see him in droves – no accounting for taste – anyway, there's been a nasty rumour going round that this is *it*.
Dora	This is what?
Vera	That *he's* the chosen one, the Messiah. The bigwigs in Jerusalem didn't want to seem too interested, so they sent Samuel and one or two others to snoop around a bit, you know, ask a few questions.
Dora	Oooh, how exciting. And . . . ?
Vera	Well, he's not . . . at least he says he's not. But obviously what he said got one or two people worried. Samuel wasn't able to make him out at all. He said that when he wasn't quoting scriptures he wasn't making any sense at all. The gist of it was that there's somebody else coming. Somebody far greater, far more important than John.
Dora	And when's this more important person coming?
Vera	That's the problem – we don't know and John wouldn't say. I think that's what's got Samuel so angry. We've got to wait.
Dora	Oooh, I hate waiting.
Vera	Not as much as Samuel. Come on, the thing to do when you've got to wait is have a nice cup of tea – come inside.

They exit.

Third Sunday of Advent Year C

Zephaniah 3.14–20   Philippians 4.4–7   Luke 3.7–18

Coming home   *Zephaniah 3.14–20*
This is a meditative monologue based on the themes of the Zephaniah passage. Quiet thoughtfulness is required in the presentation. No special costume or effects are needed.

It was on the third day of being stranded in foreign climes that he began to long for home. The queues in the airport, the lack of information, the extra expense that the insurance company definitely wouldn't reimburse – all these things played their part in his growing frustration and anxiety – but it was also greater than all of those things. He wanted, more than anything else, to go home.

As he sat, nursing the next in a seemingly endless line of cups of coffee, he began to ask himself why this might be. Why this sudden need to be home? He had never counted himself a great homemaker, he hadn't thought of himself as being overly sentimental. It was four walls, his possessions, such as they might be. It wasn't as if his home hadn't moved from one place to another over the years. So why, sat waiting for yet another depressing update of the situation with his delayed flight, did he yearn to be back there?

It was home. That was all he could come up with. It was his place on this over-crowded planet. It was stuff accumulated over the years – photos he didn't look at from one year to the next, books, some music and movies, paintings and souvenirs he'd picked up to remind himself of places he'd been, people he knew. It was familiar, it was where people knew they could contact him, it was where his post was delivered. It was home.

He wondered what all this had to say about his faith. His faith that had been so sorely tested as he stood trying to keep his cool in front of officious check-in desk staff – 'Don't lose your temper with them – it's not their fault' – he had said to himself over and over again. If home meant so much – what about asylum seekers, refugees, rootless and homeless wanderers?

He wasn't sure that he had any answers except for the fact that dredged up from somewhere, at the bottom of his mind there was the memory of a prayer. He couldn't even remember all of the words, but he was sure this phrase was in it: 'When we were still far off you met us in your Son and brought us home.' Growing up it had been one of his favourite prayers and he was surprised, now, by how easily the words came back to him . . . and he was impressed by their simple power.

Perhaps, he thought, just perhaps, finding your home in God might be enough. In fact more than enough – it might be more important than anything else.

Creed   *Philippians 4.4–7*
Creeds are both individual and corporate acts of devotion. This could be duplicated and recited by the whole group.

I believe in a God who wants us to be joyful,
to be excited by the beauty of life.
I believe in a God who wants us to open our eyes fully
to see the wonders of life that explode around us every day.
I believe that worship that doesn't reflect that joy
is but a pale example of how worship should be.
Worshipping God should be shot through with the
deep joy that pulses at the heart of creation.
I believe that God calls us to be gentle and kind
in the way that we treat this beautiful planet and each other.
In a world that celebrates selfishness and glorifies violence
I know that being gentle and celebrating kindness can
be an upsetting and challenging thing to do.
It is a radical and revolutionary way to live your life.
I believe that God wants us to be a people of prayer –
a community that has prayer at the core of its being,
asking God for everything we need.
I believe that does not mean that the answer to every prayer is 'yes'.
But as we grow closer and the relationship grows deeper
we become more and more in tune with God's love.
I believe that God does not want us to worry.
That does not mean that we won't,
but it does mean that we can rest at peace knowing God is there.
And God's peace
that is so great that we cannot understand it
will be all that we need.

The One   *Luke 3.7–18*
Two actors are sitting centrally at a table. Shaun and Tracy are caricatures and should be played as such. They are earnest and slightly self-righteous. No special costuming is needed.

Shaun	Now then, comrades, I would like to declare this meeting of the Popular People's Liberation Front of Judea officially open.
Tracy	Here, here, well said, Shaun, I'm ever so impressed.
Shaun	The meeting officially recognizes Tracy . . . thank you very much for those kind words.
Tracy	It's all so official.
Shaun	Yes, indeed it is . . . now can we get down to the topic of this evening's very important meeting?
Tracy	Oooh, yes. Shall I take minutes?
Shaun	Yes, please, comrade Tracy.
Tracy	You'd have thought that with it being such an important meeting and everything there'd be more than the two of us here.
Shaun	Numbers aren't everything.
Tracy	No – you're quite right. It's commitment and loyalty to the cause that counts . . . ain't that right, Shaun?
Shaun	Absolutely. Now there is only one matter of business before us tonight.
Tracy	But it's really important, isn't it?
Shaun	Will you stop interrupting me?
Tracy	Oh . . . sorry. But there is only the two of us here isn't there?
Shaun	That's hardly the point . . . the point is . . . is he the one or not?
Tracy	You mean John?
Shaun	Yes, I mean John.
Tracy	I just wanted to be clear . . . for the minutes. And by 'the one' I assume you mean the Messiah?
Shaun	(Getting increasingly frustrated) Yes, the Messiah. Is John the Baptizer actually the Messiah?
Tracy	Well, if he is we should support him, shouldn't we?
Shaun	That's the whole point – if he is the Messiah, then we ought to throw the whole resources of the Popular People's Liberation Front of Judea behind him.
Tracy	What, all five of us?
Shaun	We are a mighty army.
Tracy	We are indeed . . . except for my aunt Cynthia . . . she's got two walking sticks.
Shaun	(Ignoring her) There is still the question . . . is it him?
Tracy	Well, he's a bit fierce isn't he?
Shaun	And uncompromising . . . that's good, that is.

Tracy	But on the other hand his clothes are really awful, he smells of the desert, and don't even get me started on what he eats . . . locusts are so gross.
Shaun	But is he the one?
Tracy	He says he isn't.
Shaun	But he might just be saying that to lead us astray.
Tracy	I suppose.
Shaun	It's just that we've been waiting so long, and he seems so right.
Tracy	*(Slightly hesitant, but wanting to ask)* Shaun . . . do you think the Messiah is going to be how we've imagined him?
Shaun	Of course, he is . . . revolutionary, a leader.
Tracy	But what if he's a different version of those things? What if we're looking in the wrong direction?
Shaun	Not even remotely possible, Tracy. Now take down this letter . . . I'm going to write to the Governor.
Tracy	Oooh, Shaun . . . you always know the right thing to do.

Fourth Sunday of Advent Year A

Isaiah 7.10–16   Romans 1.1–7   Matthew 1.18–25

The choice   *Isaiah 7.10–16*
This is a straight meditative reading, not a monologue, and needs to be delivered with conviction and thought but not drama.

For those who know God, who see God, who hear God – there is a very simple choice that needs to be made. Simple and yet occasionally profoundly difficult.

The choice is this: If I know what God wants of me, do I do it or not?

At its most basic level the choice is very simple. If you know what God wants of you why would you not want to do it? What could be more profound, satisfying, joy-giving, than doing what you know God wants? Saying 'yes' to God must be the most liberating, the most obvious thing in all the world.

Mustn't it?

But it isn't always as simple as that.

Saying 'yes' to God means we surrender control. Saying 'yes' to God takes power away from us. Saying 'yes' to God is a massively risky exercise. No wonder Ahaz didn't want to do it. To say 'yes' was to give up so much.

And, of course, there is a difference between being uncertain and saying 'no'.

We can all understand uncertainty. There are always questions: Is it really God? How can I be sure? But to be sure and to say 'no' to God. Anyway, that is something else.

To say 'no' is to choose yourself.

To say 'no' is to claim that you know better.

To say 'no' is to turn your back on God.

We hate to give up control. We like to think that we are the centre. We don't want to hand things over. Often what God asks sounds risky, crazy, beyond our imagining.

And so, once more, we come back to the choice – simple and yet profoundly difficult. If I know what God wants of me, do I do it or not? Do I say 'yes' with all of the risk and the excitement, the uncertainty and the adventure that that entails?

What would you choose?

Good news   *Romans 1.1–7*

This brisk two-narrator sketch should be delivered slickly with speed and energy. Both actors should enter with confidence and enthusiasm (perhaps from the audience/congregation).

One	Good news!
Two	You've won the lottery?
One	No.
Two	You've found a load of money?
One	No.
Two	Your eccentric and seldom-heard-of great aunt Betty has just died and somewhat surprisingly left you millions in her will?
One	Well, now you're just being silly.
Two	Oh, I don't know . . . it's possible.
One	Still no – and by the way . . . why do all your guesses involve money?
Two	You said there was good news didn't you? That means money as far as I'm concerned.
One	Well, this good news *is* about a gift – but it's way more important than money.
Two	So somebody has given you something.
One	And you . . . in fact everybody.
Two	What everybody in this room?

One	Everybody in the world.
Two	Wait a minute . . . let me see if I've got this right. You're telling me that everybody in the world has been given something that is more important than loads of money.
One	Correct.
Two	What on earth is this fantastic gift then?
One	Jesus.
Two	Jesus?
One	Promised through the ages, foretold by prophets, come to earth as a human being . . . God's gift to us.
Two	But . . .
One	Ah you see that's the problem with people in our 'oh so clever' world. There's always a 'but'. 'But' do we need him? 'But' how do we know? God has given us the most precious gift ever – and we respond with 'but'.
Two	That's not being very grateful, is it?
One	No . . . it's not.
Two	I need to learn more.
One	That's a good response.
Two	I need to think this through.
One	That's good too. Me? *Pause.* I'm going to worship.

The conversation   *Matthew 1.18–25*

Joseph and his best friend David are sitting centrally. They are clearly comfortable telling each other the truth with warmth. No special staging or costumes are needed. A sentence or two of introduction might help in setting the scene.

David	Look Joseph . . . how long have we known each other?
Joseph	Since we were little kids.
David	Right . . . we've been through a lot together – thick and thin. So I think I've earned the right to say this – Joseph, if you do this you are being an idiot, a plonker, the world's biggest twit.
Joseph	Oh, thanks!
David	Well, what am I supposed to say? You're not making any sense.
Joseph	I'm just so confused.
David	You're confused? How do you think Mary feels?
Joseph	Look – the divorce would be done secretly, quietly.

David	It's still a divorce.
Joseph	Well, look at what's happened!
David	Okay, about what's happened . . . as I understand it, Mary has given you her explanation.
Joseph	If you can call it an explanation!
David	Ah, well, you see there's your problem. Look, as far as I see it there is only one question that you need to be asking yourself.
Joseph	Oh yeah . . . and what's that?
David	Do I trust her?
Joseph	But . . .
David	No – no 'ifs', no 'buts' – do I trust her? Look, Joseph, we both remember what you were like, don't we? Do I have to remind you? Because I will . . .
Joseph	Well, I . . .
David	You were hardly the world's greatest catch. Talk about a man of few words – you could barely string a sentence together. Painfully shy and with very few prospects. And then you met Mary.
Joseph	It was . . .
David	Magical? Amazing? Stupendous? I hate to say it, Joseph, because it doesn't say much for what a friend I've been – but I'm telling you that since you've met Mary you're a better – a changed – person. Everybody says so.
Joseph	I suppose I am.
David	No supposing about it – fact. So we come back to that all-important question – if Mary has never given you any reason to doubt anything she's ever said, why would you start now? Always reminding yourself, of course, that we're talking about Mary, the most devout, lovely, holy person that either of us knows.
Joseph	It's just been so difficult.
David	I know, mate, I know. But I know Mary, and more importantly I know you. And I can't help but feel that something . . . something really important is going on here. Come on.

They exit.

Fourth Sunday of Advent Year B

2 Samuel 7.1–11, 16   Romans 16.25–7   Luke 1.26–38

Meditation   *2 Samuel 7.1–11, 16*

The atmosphere of this narrative meditation should be that of somebody telling a story. A standard lamp and armchair could be used.

'A tent or a temple?' she asked, firmly but politely. 'It may seem like a strange question, an unimportant one, but actually it's vital. How does God dwell among his people? Where do we go looking for God? Where is God to be found? Sometimes, I'll admit,' she continued, 'I want God to live in a tent, because a tent is just right, isn't it? Always ready to move to where it's needed. Mobile, flexible, not expensive or gaudy or set in stone. A dwelling that can be put up or taken down quickly, respond to need, a lifestyle that takes on only what's required – all the unnecessary stuff that we surround ourselves with can't be carried and is thrown away. A radical, different kind of a place, a tent; it's edgy, quirky. It's all the things that I want God to be . . . sometimes.' She shifted in her chair, squirmed impatiently. She was obviously not entirely content with what she had just said. There was something else.

'But then sometimes I want the opposite. I want God to dwell in a temple. After all, God is unchangeable, great, powerful, almighty, majestic. God can't be held by our human ideas. God is so outside . . . beyond all of our ideas that how on earth could a tent do justice to what we want to say? No the only place that God could possibly dwell is in a great temple – a marvellous building that points towards the heavens. A building full of the greatest offerings that humanity has to offer, the most incredible craftsmanship, the most creative and imaginative ideas. A temple helps us by its glory to focus our ideas, turn our thoughts to things above and beyond us.'

She shifted in her seat again. 'So which is it? A temple or a tent? How does God dwell with us? How does God come to be with people?'

The wise, old one smiled at the girl and leant forward. 'A temple or a tent you ask? I am very glad to say it is neither . . . God dwells with us in the shape of a person . . . a man after God's own heart.'

Monologue   **Romans 16.25–7**

This dramatic monologue takes the form of a magician sharing his/her thoughts. The style should be warm and conversational. No special costume or effects are needed.

I've been in the business of magic for a long time now. My job is to stun and amaze you. By sleight of hand, by misdirection, by making your mind believe what your eyes are seeing, I can turn your beliefs about the world upside down. A nine-year-old boy came to me once and asked a question. He'd just got his first magic set and wanted to know what was the most important thing he could learn about magic. I looked at him very hard. There was bundled up in him all of the enthusiasm, all of the excitement and eagerness of youth. Did I dare tell him that the most important thing had nothing to do with magic at all? I took a deep breath and spoke.

'Look – the most important thing that you can learn actually has very little to do with magic at all. It's got nothing to do with bits of rope or playing cards or disappearing coins. It's this – you have got to learn timing. And before you think that's an easy thing – it isn't. Learning when is the right time and the wrong time is the most difficult and subtle thing that you can learn. You see, for everything there's an ideal time. A time when something should be hidden, unknown, perhaps even a mystery, and then the time comes when that mystery needs to be revealed, understood, grasped and seen clearly. Knowing when that time has come – knowing when the secret needs to become known, when the hidden needs to be discovered – is the most important thing to discover.'

I am not at all sure that he understood what I was trying to say, in fact I think he looked a little disappointed. That doesn't mean that what I told him isn't true. Everything – the most important events in the history of the universe – all of them have their time, the time when it is right that they should happen. The right time, the ideal time, is absolutely everything – the time when the mystery needs to become clear, the hidden comes into the light of day, the revelation takes place. The right time . . . it's one of the most important things in the world.

Breaking news   *Luke 1.26–38*
An angel is sitting centrally – another angel enters – the seated angel speaks. Angel 1 is enthusiastic and impatient. Angel 2 is more controlled and calm. No special costume is needed, but if you want to add halos it will bring a smile!

Angel 1	So, how did it go? How did she take it? Is it going to be all right? Come on, out with it!
Angel 2	Calm down, keep your halo on. She actually took it very well considering.
Angel 1	Well – I'm amazed. You could knock me down with one of your wing feathers. I mean it's not exactly easy news to hear, is it?

Angel 2	About the most difficult thing ever. Oh, hello Mary – I'm an angel of the Lord, and by the way you're going to have a child, and he's going to be the chosen one, God's own Messiah.
Angel 1	So what happened?
Angel 2	Well, I just kind of appeared and told her what was what.
Angel 1	Had she ever seen an angel before?
Angel 2	I don't suppose so, no.
Angel 1	Well, that's got to be a bit of a shock just by itself. Getting back from the shops or something, you sit down to make yourself a nice cup of tea and take the load off your feet, and suddenly there's an angel standing in front of you.
Angel 2	It's enough to make you drop your cup. And yet, as I say, she was amazingly calm about it – I got the feeling that all she *really* wanted was to do whatever God asked her to.
Angel 1	I suppose that's why she was chosen . . . why she's the right one.
Angel 2	Out of so many others who could have been selected – *she's* the one. It's amazing when you think about it.
Angel 1	The one who is really willing to do whatever God asks.
Angel 2	The next few months are going to be incredibly difficult for her.
Angel 1	Do you think she realizes that?
Angel 2	I think she'll cope – but I don't think she's got much idea of how bad things could be, no.
Angel 1	I'll send down a couple of minor cherubs to keep an eye on her.
Angel 2	That might be a good idea.
Angel 1	The scandal, the gossip, the wagging tongues – oh it's too much. I just wish there was something more we could do.
Angel 2	I'm afraid this is something she's going to have to cope with by herself – though she has got Joseph.
Angel 1	That reminds me . . . how's he taking it?
Angel 2	Well, funny you should ask that, but that's my little task for next week. I've got to go down there and give him a few pointers about standing by his woman.
Angel 1	They're certainly keeping you busy.
Angel 2	Well, as they say, 'No rest for the wicked' . . . oops, slip of the tongue . . . sorry.

Fourth Sunday of Advent Year C

Micah 5.2–5a   Hebrews 10.5–10   Luke 1.39–45 (46–55)

The significance of small things   Micah 5.2–5a

This dramatic monologue forms some imagined thoughts of Micah. It should be delivered with restrained, deep feeling. No special costuming is necessary but lighting to emphasize the reader would be helpful.

Good morning . . . look, I know it's obscure . . . you don't have to tell me that, I already know. Sometimes the words just come. It's really difficult to explain. They break over me like waves crashing on a beach and I just find myself writing them down in a bit of a daze. I finish the writing, I put down the pen and then I bend over the page to look at what I've written. Sometimes I look at the words, and it's not that I don't have any memory of writing them – I know I did – it's just that I feel slightly detached from them. It's as if they're rather remote – somebody else's thoughts. There have been occasions when I've looked at what I've written – and I have no idea what it means. It's not that the words themselves don't make any sense – they always do – I just don't know what they mean – what they're getting at.

That was especially true the day I wrote about Bethlehem. It's a backwater really, dusty, rocky, difficult and small. The most important thing about Bethlehem is that David was born there. Imagine my surprise, then, when the words that are given to me make it clear that the task of Bethlehem is not yet over. Why would God want to continue bringing glory to that tiny, strange little place? There are so many other towns – grander, more picturesque, better placed – why should it be Bethlehem? What is it about that town in particular? And, perhaps, more importantly, what is the task that still awaits it? How will God work through Bethlehem again? The words talk about a ruler. Not just any ruler, you understand, but a truly great ruler. One who will be significant in ways I cannot even begin to imagine. But, as usual, there are many questions unanswered, many parts of the picture that remain shady and vague.

What I am left with more than anything else is an overwhelming sense of the significance of small things. When you think about it, why should Bethlehem expect anything? It's not special in any way. It's small, dirty and unpleasant – except for the undeniable fact that God chooses in infinite wisdom and curious love to bring not one but two mighty rulers from this little place.

Of course, then I am left with the most amazing, life-changing truth to ponder: if God chooses to use the smallness of Bethlehem in that incredible way . . . what might God plan to do with the little love, faith and willingness that I have to offer day by day?

The meeting place   *Hebrews 10.5–10*
This narrative meditation should be delivered as if telling a story – perhaps using an armchair. No special lighting or costuming is necessary.

The old man sat quietly in his rocking chair as the warm evening breeze ruffled his hair. He looked out over the immense lake and watched as the sun set in a blaze of golden fire over the water. He sat, alone with his thoughts for a moment until he became aware of a presence behind him. 'What are you still doing up?' he asked as his grandson perched on the top of the decking and took up watch with him.

'I wanted to be with you,' came the reply.

The old man smiled gently to himself. When he was a child he had cherished similar moments with his grandfather. 'All right then, but if you're going to sit there you can help me solve a problem that's been on my mind.' The boy looked round, intrigued. 'Is there a meeting point between heaven and earth?' the old man asked.

The young boy looked puzzled. He was at the age when the only thing that made sense to him was the physical world. He devoured books on dinosaurs, machinery and how things worked. He had less time for stories – he had cast them aside as childish. Unless it could be weighed, measured or explained he had little interest. The question, to him, sounded dangerously like nonsense.

'I just wondered,' continued the old man, 'because it seems to me that would be a very special place – a place where earth and heaven meet each other. And before you start thinking that I mean the horizon over there where the sunlight touches the water – I don't. What if there was a point where the two intermingled? Where the spiritual world reached out and intersected with the physical world? What if there was a point where things earthly and things heavenly met? And what if that point where they met, where they came into focus, was not a place but a person?'

The boy did not understand and said so. He was growing tired of what he considered to be riddles and began to make his way back inside. As he did so he looked down at his grandfather's hand and there, laying in his palm, worn with age and with much handling, was a small, rough, wooden cross.

The visit   Luke 1.39–45 (46–55)
In the following sketch Zechariah does not speak but holds up a series of cards with words or symbols on them. Elizabeth is a very talkative but basically good-natured presence. No special costuming or effects are necessary.

Elizabeth	*(Calling)* Zechariah? Zechariah! Where is that man? I swear he's going to be the death of me . . . that is if I don't kill him first. *(He enters and waves)* Ah . . . there you are. So . . . where have you been? Lolling around again no doubt? Feeling sorry for yourself. Well, you've only got yourself to blame. If you had shown a little bit more faith then everything would be all right. But oh no, not my Zechariah. It was an angel, you silly man. Most people when confronted with an angel of God would just believe everything it said. After all, seeing an angel of the Lord is hardly an everyday occurrence, is it? It's not like we're running into them every day of the week. So when faced with an angel, you show the proper respect and most importantly you believe what it says. But not my husband, oh no. My husband has to question the angel, doubt its motives, think that he knows better. And look where that's got us. Although I have to say being able to get a word in edgeways for the past few months has been quite a pleasant change.
Zechariah	'?'
Elizabeth	A question mark? Why a question mark? Oh yes you wanted to know why I called you. *(He smiles and nods)* Mary's coming.
Zechariah	'?'
Elizabeth	It's always questions with, you, isn't it. I should have listened to my Mother. 'Don't marry him,' she said, 'he's a questioner,' she said . . . she was right. Mary – my cousin – from Nazareth. She's coming here to visit. Yes, I know we don't see very much of them, but it's nice of her to call. It's a long journey, and you've got to be nice. She's had a hard time recently, and you're not to mention it. Oh wait a minute . . . I forgot . . . you can't mention it. Something's gone on in Nazareth, and I'm not quite sure what, but you hear rumours – always rumours. And these ones aren't very nice.
Zechariah	'?'
Elizabeth	There's something wrong with her betrothal. I never did like that Joseph, never trust a carpenter, my mother used to tell me. Anyway, it's beginning to sound as though they're sending her here to get her out of the way. Three months they want her to stay here . . . three months. I mean, she's a lovely girl, I've got nothing against her. But three months is enough to try anybody's patience. And that amount of time . . . well, you've just got to wonder whether there's some reason they need her gone for a while, that's all I'm saying.

Zechariah	'Angel.' '?'
Elizabeth	You're seeing angels everywhere at the moment, aren't you. What . . . you mean she's seen an angel? Oh don't be silly. You really are the most ridiculous man. Why would Mary have seen an angel? I mean I know you were told that our baby was going to be special . . . you don't mean? *(He nods)* Mary's pregnant too? Oh . . . I'd better go and tell the servants to prepare. Well, don't just stand there you silly man, come and help.
She exits.	
Zechariah	'!'
Elizabeth	*(Bellowing from offstage)* Zechariah!
He exits.	

2

Christingle

Christingle 1

Candles

Two actors stand centrally. There is no need to identify that they are candles in terms of costumes but a sentence of introduction to the idea might be helpful.

Pamela	You know what, Rodney?
Rodney	What's that then, Pamela?
Pamela	I hate this time of year.
Rodney	So do I – with a vengeance.
Pamela	I mean, everybody's full of festive cheer.
Rodney	Peace and goodwill to all.
Pamela	But when you're a candle . . .
Rodney	Yes, when you're a candle . . .
Pamela	It's miserable . . .
Rodney	Depressing.
Pamela	The only thing worse would be if you were a turkey.
Rodney	Yeah, I don't suppose they're looking forward to Christmas either.
Pamela	But being a candle is such a pain at Christmas.
Rodney	Particularly when you're small candles like us.
Pamela	I mean, if you were a big, chunky, slow-burning candle . . .
Rodney	Then they'd put you out front and you'd be there for all to see.
Pamela	If you were a mid-sized candle . . .
Rodney	You might get put in the Advent Ring.
Pamela	That would be nice. And if you were one of those huge novelty candles with three wicks that looks like a train . . .
Rodney	The chances are you'd never get lit at all.
Pamela	Nah – you'd just get stuck on a mantelpiece 'cos nobody's sure which wick to light first, or how you're going to burn.

Rodney	Or they say, 'Oooh what a lovely novelty candle, it seems a shame to light it, let's put it over here on the bookcase instead.'
Pamela	But no, when you're small candles like us . . .
Rodney	The chances are that the cruellest torture of all awaits you.
Pamela	Yes, the likeliest is they're going to do the worst thing that they can do to any candle.
Rodney	A fate worse than death.
Pamela	They're going to put you into . . . a Christingle.
Rodney	Oh, the shame! All that orange juice squirting around your bottom.
Pamela	All those cocktail sticks with huge amounts of sweets on them.
Rodney	They light you for about a minute.
Pamela	And then they blow you out – muttering something about health and safety and risk assessments.
Rodney	And then they proceed to stuff themselves with the sweets.
Pamela	Of course, as soon as you've been blown out and the sweets have been eaten, what use are you?
Rodney	What use are you?
Pamela	None at all.
Rodney	The interest has completely disappeared.
Pamela	After all, who wants to eat an orange with candle wax on it?
Rodney	So we get thrown away.
Pamela	Tossed aside like an old boot!
Rodney	Oh, the indignity of it all.
Pamela	Oh, the shame.
Rodney	So this is our fate this year.
Pamela	Miserable, isn't it?
Rodney	*(Leans forward and listens)* Wait a minute, did you hear that?
Pamela	What?
Rodney	The preacher . . . he just mentioned us.
Pamela	*(Excited)* Did he? What did he say?
Rodney	He said we're the most important part of the whole Christingle.
Pamela	Important? Us? How?
Rodney	He said that we represent Jesus – who came as a light, into a very dark world.
Pamela	So we *are* important. I knew it!
Rodney	So no matter how dark the world becomes . . .
Pamela	And however lonely and hopeless it sometimes seems . . .
Rodney	A light always shines.

Pamela	And the darkness cannot put it out.
Rodney	So let your light shine.
Pamela	Just like ours!

Christingle 2

The marketing meeting

Two actors stand with a flip chart or large graph. Les and Jess are dressed smartly and are caricatures of a certain kind of sales/marketing person – all certainty laced with a complete lack of understanding.

Jess	So then, Les, what have we got?
Les	Well, Jess, as you know, our focus groups have been telling us that they think Christmas has become too commercialized. They're sick of seeing stockings and cards in the shops in August, they're tired of hearing carols from early November – they want something new, something that speaks of the real spirit of Christmas. Something that makes them feel good about themselves.
Jess	And that's just what we're going to give them . . . at a price, of course. So, you've been looking at what Christians do around Christmas to see how we can make some money out of it. Is that right?
Les	Absolutely.
Jess	Tell me again, why Christians?
Les	Well, it's because it's *their* festival.
Jess	It is? Well, you learn something new every day on this job.
Les	Anyway, after extensive research I've come up with the perfect product. It takes a favourite traditional symbol of Christmas and it tweaks it just a little so we can make large amounts of dosh on it.
Jess	And this symbol is?
Les	Right here. *(Takes out Christingle)* It's called a CHRIS . . . tingle.
Jess	*(Looking at it)* So what does it do?
Les	Well, our research tells us you light the candle and then you eat the sweets.
Jess	Is that it?
Les	Well, there's something about the candle representing the light of the world or something.

Jess	What about the red ribbon?
Les	Well, apparently that's about the blood of Jesus.
Jess	Eurgh! We're going to have to lose that. What on earth do these Christians think they're doing? Blood at Christmas? Who wants that?
Les	I know . . . weird, isn't it?
Jess	Okay, here's what I'm thinking. First we lose the fruit.
Les	What, the orange?
Jess	Absolutely. They're messy and smelly and the most important thing is that the profit margin is awful. We replace it with a plastic orange which splits in the middle and has a little plastic toy inside. Missiles and tanks for the boys, little dolly things with bad hair for the girls.
Les	That's a great idea.
Jess	We lose the red ribbon and replace it with a tattoo glitter-strip that you can peel off the plastic orange and attach round your wrist as a fashion accessory. How cool is that?
Les	You're a genius. What about the sweets? They're meant to represent the fruits of the Spirit or something like that.
Jess	Perfect, with talk of spirits we can launch it at Hallowe'en. But this candle has got to go. Naked flame . . . I mean, think of all the lawsuits.
Les	Nightmare. What about a funky little glow-strip thing? One of those that you snap and it glows fluorescent for an hour or so.
Jess	Great. Oh, this is so much better than what the Christians have. Sweets, a toy, fashion accessories and a glow-strip.
Les	What would it retail for?
Jess	Well, we can source all the materials for around 50p.
Les	So I'm thinking £5.99.
Jess	Oh, at least. It'll be the new must-have toy for the Christmas season.
Les	Every parent will have to buy one for their kiddies' stockings.
Jess	We can market it as being retro cool so the teenagers will think they've got to have one as well.
Les	We're onto a goldmine here.
Jess	And the best thing is, it's all about the true spirit of Christmas.
Les	Oh, absolutely. We've left the spirit of the thing completely intact. Cash registers here we come!

Christingle 3

Robert and Katy on Christingles

Robert and Katy are seven-year-olds played by adults. They are eager and enthu-
siastic. You can either dress the two actors appropriately or give a short sentence
of introduction.

Robert	*(Very excited)* Can't wait, can't wait, can't wait!
Katy	*(Entering)* What are you so excited about, then?
Robert	Only the best church service of the whole year.
Katy	What d'ya mean?
Robert	Well, like, most church services are really boring, aren't they? It's all talk, talk, talk, be a better person, do this, don't do that, yack, yack, yack, yack.
Katy	So what's so different this week, then?
Robert	Don't you know nothing? This week's the Christingle service.
Katy	Ah, cool.
Robert	Exactly . . . cool. The only service of the year when I get to play with a naked flame!
Katy	Last year you nearly set fire to Pamela Smeakley's coat.
Robert	*(Remembering)* Oh yeah, that was great.
Katy	Except for the fact that your Dad stopped sweet privileges for a whole three days.
Robert	*(Suddenly serious)* That was the longest three days of my life.
Katy	Do we get to make our Christingles at home again this year?
Robert	I think so. Dad said the grown-ups at church were tired of getting the juice from 120 oranges sprayed over their hands.
Katy	That's better, 'cos that means we get to put our own sweets on. When they make them at church they're really mingy sweet-wise.
Robert	And we can pile them REALLY high.
Katy	Last year you couldn't see my orange for the sweets.
Robert	My Christingle had 27 sweets on . . . I counted.
Katy	Well, mine had a . . . a zillion and six on.
Robert	That's impossible.
Katy	No it isn't . . . I counted them.
Robert	Anyway – what with the sweets and the naked flame – that makes Christingle my favourite service of the whole year.
Katy	And it's all about Jesus.

Robert	Is it?
Katy	Of course it is. Honestly, you're so dim sometimes.
Robert	Well, how is it about Jesus then?
Katy	Well, the orange is the world.
Robert	But the world isn't orange . . . it's blue and green and things . . . I've seen a photo.
Katy	Well, it's not *actually* the world, is it? It's a symbol.
Robert	Isn't that a thing that makes a great crashing sound when you play it?
Katy	Yeah, I think so.
Robert	So how come the world's like that then?
Katy	I don't know – it's adult stuff. *(Carrying on)* The candle is the light of Jesus.
Robert	Even when it sets light to Pamela Smeakley's coat?
Katy	No, that's just you being you. Then the red ribbon is for the blood of Jesus.
Robert	Going all round the world.
Katy	Exactly, and the sweets are . . .
Robert	The sweets are for me.
Katy	I know that, but they stand for something.
Robert	Who cares? They're for me.
Katy	Now, is it the four corners of the world? Or the fruits of the earth? Or the fruits of the Spirit?
Robert	Can't it be all of them as long as I get to eat them?
Katy	I suppose so.
Robert	Cool.
Katy	My mum says that the most important part of Christingle is to remember what it stands for.
Robert	My dad says it's a message that you hold in your hand.
Katy	I think our parents are quite clever really.
Robert	Absolutely. And when we sing the carol with all the candles glowing, it's really pretty.
Katy	I think that's why it's my favourite service of the whole year.
Robert	And there's the sweets.
Katy	Oh yes – there's always the sweets.

3

Christmas

Christmas Day Year A

Isaiah 9.2–7   Titus 2.11–14   Luke 2.1–14 (15–20)

The message   *Isaiah 9.2–7*
Two actors stand centrally. No special costuming is necessary, but the piece needs to be delivered with a sense of awe and wonder.

One	We really, honestly, truthfully could have done nothing to earn it . . .
Two	Be worthy of it . . .
One	Deserve it.
Two	But that's the best thing about it.
One	He is given for us anyway . . .
Two	Born *for* us . . .
One	Wonderful counsellor . . .
Two	Mighty God . . .
One	Everlasting Father . . .
Two	Prince of Peace . . .
One	Could it be any better?
Two	Any more perfect?
One	What we needed more than anything else . . .
Two	God has given to us.
One	There is no way in which we can ever be worthy of the gift.
Two	But it is given anyway.
One	Out of the most amazing and breath-taking love.
Two	And when we are tempted to be down-hearted . . .
One	To lack love or hope . . .

Two	To think that the world is lost.
One	All we need to do is come back to these words and allow their truth to seep deep down into our weary hearts.
Two	For they make clear to us the most important thing in all the world.
One	The God who exists beyond time and space and has created everything there is – loves us.
Two	And has acted to save us and bring us hope.
One	In Jesus we see.
Two	In Jesus we understand.
One	In Jesus – the relationship of love is sealed.

Meditation   *Titus 2.11–14*

This meditation may be too hard-hitting for Christmas-morning family services but would work at a Christmas-Eve communion. It can easily be delivered by more than one voice.

It is not enough.
It has never been enough.
Sometimes we have succeeded in deluding ourselves, thinking that we have somehow pleased God.
Singing our carols, going to the Christmas concert seemed like a good idea.
We enjoyed the nativity play and the Christingle service.
But if we really sit down to analyse – to think seriously about what we've done and why . . .
then we realize that perhaps we've done them all because *we* enjoy them.
We love the warm and cosy glow they give us.
The satisfaction of doing well-loved things – the cosy glow of nostalgia.
But looking at the manger and picturing lowing cattle and donkeys gently nuzzling has never been enough.
If we look at the cradle and all we see is a baby being born then we have succeeded in keeping Jesus locked up,
kept him from making an impact, succeeded in protecting ourselves again.
If what we say about Christmas is true – if it really is about 'God and sinners reconciled'.
If God is doing in Jesus what the carols proclaim . . .
Well, then it changes everything, doesn't it?

Absolutely everything is different.
Shot through with new potential, new hope, new glory.
And that changes everything – including, inconveniently enough, the way
we live.
The things we think, the words we say, the attitudes we take.
Everything changes.
How could it not?
For that baby born in Bethlehem and placed in a manger
cracks the universe open with his first cry.
Hope and love stream into the world.
Salvation comes.
For this baby is God.
Born to raise the sons of earth.
Born to give them second birth.

The memo   *Luke 2.1–14 (15–20)*
The entirety of this piece should be read as if being delivered to a board meeting.
The actor ought to be dressed smartly.

Memo: To Wesley Taylor (CEO of Knicky Knacks Products)
Re: Christmas Sales
Regarding this year's Christmas sales I can provide you with the figures up to
and including December 19th, and it looks like it's been another record year. We
put out the first Christmas stock of cards and gift paper in June – just to raise the
profile of the festive season with our customers. Although we didn't sell any until
October, it's always good to get our stuff out ahead of the competition. Sales were
soon brisk. Heavy marketing running through December of our new range of war
toys was very effective. Our slogan, 'Sometimes peace and goodwill come with a
price', seemed to work splendidly for our range of realistic guns, grenades, ba-
zookas and armoured personnel carriers. Another big seller for us this year was
our 'Shop till you drop' range of dolls for girls. Each doll comes with its own credit
card, personal shopper and bank overdraft letter. We have managed to persuade
girls in the 8- to 12- year-old category nationwide that the only cool thing to do is
wander round shops buying things you can't afford. That should be very profitable
for us in the years to come.

I should perhaps mention that a week ago our sales office received a letter that
has frankly mystified us. It appears to have been sent by a Christian in Chester-
field attacking us for destroying the true meaning of Christmas and trivializing

a religious festival. I'm really not quite sure what they're talking about. I know Christians have some Church festival around this time of year but they're not celebrating anything in particular are they? The letter mentioned something about a baby being born for peace and salvation, and there being some kind of good news for the poor. That's hardly going to lift our sales at this time of year, is it? I suggest we ignore this complaint completely and get on with what we've been doing every Christmas at Knicky Knacks for the past 40 years, and that is getting people to part with as much money as possible over as long a period as possible.
Merry Christmas.
E. J. Cranston – Head of Sales, Knicky Knacks

Christmas Day Year B

Isaiah 62.6–12   Titus 3.4–7   Luke 2.(1–7) 8–20

The watchmen   *Isaiah 62.6–12*
Roy stands centrally, looking eagerly into the distance, and is an enthusiastic presence throughout. Gary is more worldly-wise and can enter from his place in the audience/congregation.

Roy	Come on, come on, come on. Hurry up. *(Looks at his watch)* There isn't much time left . . . not much time at all. Oh come on. *(Enter Gary)*
Gary	Morning Roy. I'm here.
Roy	Oh no.
Gary	Oh thank you very much . . . what a lovely welcome! Not, 'It's lovely to see you, Gary. Thank you for being on time for your shift Gary.' Just, 'Oh no.' Well, thanks a bunch. I know when I'm not welcome.
Roy	O Gary – look you know I don't mean it. I'm happy to see you. You know that.
Gary	Well, you could have fooled me Roy.
Roy	It's just that I love being a watchman so much – always eager, always at the ready, always watching. And last night I was sure it was going to happen. Just as the sun came up over the mountains over there I thought . . . it's happening – get ready to shout it out, to let everybody know, to bellow it out at the top of your scarily loud voice . . . but it didn't.

Gary	Well, I'm glad you enjoy your job so much Roy. It must be lovely to be so committed to your chosen profession. But I'm here now, so you can go home and get some sleep. I'll see you tonight.
Roy	You know what . . . I don't think I can.
Gary	Can what?
Roy	Sleep, Gary . . . sleep. Can't sleep. What it if happens while I'm asleep? That would never do. Knowing my luck, I'll put my head down for 40 winks, I'll just nod off and it'll happen. Just in that 30 minutes when I've got my eyes closed. I can't let that happen, Gary, I just can't. It's my job to watch, to wait, to be ready when the time comes, and that's what I'm going to do.
Gary	But you can't do that forever Roy.
Roy	It's not going to be forever Gary, is it? It's going to happen, and it's going to happen soon. I can feel it in me bones – and I've got to be ready.
Gary	Okay, okay. If you're that sure pull up a chair by me and we'll watch together.
Roy	Thanks Gary – the king's on his way. The kingdom's coming.
Gary	I hope you're right Roy.
Roy	I know I am Gary. I know I am. Pass me one of those yummy custard creams would you?

What it takes   *Titus 3.4–7*
This meditation should be delivered with real conviction, but it is not a dramatic monologue and should not be treated as such.

I love Christmas – snowmen and robins and cards and trees and decorations and presents and holly and mistletoe and nativity plays and turkey and tinsel and stockings and Father Christmas. I love it all – every nostalgia-soaked moment of it. I love the build-up (as long as it doesn't start too early mind you). I love all the things that nestle alongside it as traditions. I love it. But not as much as I love what I know it tells me about God.

There are countless images and they're all different. Loving shepherds, a serene mother dressed in blue and white, a group of wide-eyed farm animals. All those artists have all been grasping for something, all trying to convey a sense. But how do you picture what was happening on that night? As shepherds encounter God on a hillside, as a baby is born in a shed – heaven cracks open. How do you convey what is really going on? Do you even try?

I still don't pretend to understand it myself – how it is possible. But in some way, in some glorious, unexpected, challenging, love-soaked way, God comes to us. And I love what Christmas tells me about God. It tells me that the creator of the entire universe, with all its billions of galaxies stars and planets, cares so much about me, loves me so much that a child is sent into this world. A child is sent to live exactly the same kind of life that I live, with all its joy and sadness. That child does that so that God can understand what it is like to be me. So that God can create a relationship with me, better understand me – save me from all that threatens to tear me down. Christmas tells me that God has poured out love for me and everyone on this planet in great gushing streams of grace-filled joy.

I love Christmas and all its traditions – I really do – but I love even more what Christmas tells me about the God who is prepared to do all of that for me.

The innkeeper   *Luke 2.(1–7) 8–20*

This dramatic monologue is the imagined thoughts of the Bethlehem innkeeper who found room. Do not worry about the deliberate anachronisms – they only add to the fun. The important thing is the rather self-important air of hospitality giving.

Ah good morning, good morning. Welcome to Bethlehem. I am your host. Mr Joshua Goodley, proprietor of this fine establishment – The Bethlehem Travellers Rest. I can guarantee accommodations of the finest quality. Camel and donkey valet parking is round the back. All our rooms include tea- and coffee-making facilities and a complimentary packet of biscuits and small container of shampoo. A mini-bar service is available in select rooms. *(Pause to listen to customer)*. Oh but, of course: you're interested in what happened here 30 years ago. Well, let me tell you, it was a night that I will not forget in a hurry. You know, I'm sure, that Bethlehem was a nightmare that year. Census guests everywhere, nobody had booked ahead to get our most attractive rates. Well, we were almost ready to close up for the night when this poor-looking desperate chap turns up at the desk. White as a sheet he was. His . . . ah . . . lady friend . . . (shall we put it?) was sitting on a donkey outside. Now I'm no medical expert, although I do have my First Aiders proficiency badge, but even I could tell she was about to have a baby.

I felt so sorry for them. Nothing I could do on the room front – there really wasn't. But there was just something about them. And, well . . . you are looking at the worlds' biggest softie . . . I showed them our spacious animal husbandry area at the back (otherwise known as the shed). And once I had got them to sign away all liability issues on the part of the establishment, I left to settle down for what I could feel in my bones was going to be a difficult night.

And I was right – that wasn't the end of it. Oh dear me, no. About 2 a.m. there was a knock on the desk. Knock, knock, knock – as loud as you like. Well, I worried about the other guests being disturbed – we are a quiet and discreet establishment here, only the very nicest clientele. Anyway – I came out of my office and there stood the roughest group of shepherds you have ever seen in your life. They looked like they'd just seen a ghost, or something, and I swear one of them was shaking. They asked me where the baby was and I pointed them to the shed and they left, taking their stinky lambs with them. I could have sworn I heard one of them muttering something about angels as they left.

Anyway, so there you have it. It doesn't seem like 30 year ago now. It really doesn't. Joseph his name was and I think her name was Mary. Over the last year or so people, like you, have started coming in asking about it. Apparently the baby is now all grown up and making a bit of a name for himself. But I ask you – with that kind of start in life you can't expect very much . . . can you?

Christmas Day Year C

Isaiah 52.7–10   Hebrews 1.1–4   John 1.1–14

Good news   *Isaiah 52.7–10*
This poem can be delivered by more than one voice if required and should be performed with bright certainty.

The problem is that we've forgotten what good news is.
We think it's got something to do with money.
So it's good news if you win the lottery, or your horse comes in.
It's good news if you inherit something or win a competition.
And while all of those might be good news
They are in the end
Very small.
Whereas
The good news that God offers us on Christmas Day
Is immense

HUGE
It tells us that God has come.
Come into the creation that divine hands created
Come in tiny, wrinkled, vulnerable form.
Come to save,
To bring peace,
Joy,
Grace,
Love.
To save us from ourselves.
It tells us that God's purpose is to share the divine life with us
And that nothing else will do.
There will be no second-hand copies,
No weak imitations.
God has come
Has shared,
Has rescued,
Has forgiven,
Has brought us home.
Now THAT is good news
Worth shouting from the mountain tops
Announcing from street corners
Proclaiming from pulpits.
God loves us and has come to us
In human form.
Amen.

Angel talk   *Hebrews 1.1–4*
Sarah is warm, chatty and deeply lovable. No special costume is necessary. She could enter from the audience/congregation in character.

Oh, hello, goodness look at all of you. How exciting – and how festive you all look. Bless. Well, my name's Sarah – and I'm an angel. Not that I'm well behaved or anything – although I do try my best . . . no, I actually am an angel. You know the sort, wings, halos, tinsel . . . yes, like that . . . only not a lot like that. Goodness, now I'm getting myself all muddled up, and I promised I wouldn't. We're just not what you'll have pictured – that's all . . . *(Indicates herself)* as you can see.

Well – a happy Christmas to you all. Exciting, isn't it? I remember the first one. What's that? I don't look old enough? Well, bless you for caring. That's lovely. And that night . . . well, I just never seem to tire of talking about it . . . I really don't. I don't mean talking about what happened, although that was special enough. After all, we don't often take the whole choir down. I mean there are so many of us and, such a nightmare getting everybody ready and looking their best. And the shepherds – bless them – they were in such a state. Mouths hanging open in amazement, cowering behind rocks – well, it's not every day you see and hear the heavenly choir, is it? It was wonderful and exciting and joyful and lovely . . . it really was lovely. But that's not the bit that I never get tired of talking about, it really isn't – special though it was.

The bit that really does take my breath away even after all these years is the meaning behind what was going on. We were told – of course we were told – what was happening. That God – the almighty God – had gone to earth, had sent the Son to be born in a cattle shed, but we could hardly believe it was happening. You will never understand the glory of that act – the sheer amazing love of it. It was extraordinary – that God should do that. We were so excited. It meant that healing and love and forgiveness and new beginnings were going to be made possible. It meant that you – yes all of you – have the possibility of a new relationship with God. Oooh, the wonder of it.

That's why I never get tired of talking about it. It means so much – this most glorious, loving, precious and costly gift. I do hope the wonder dawns upon you with new power this Christmas. Anyway, I must go. As I said, a happy Christmas to you all. And by the way, sir, I do love your tie . . . was it a gift? *(Pause)* Have you got the receipt?

The presents   *John 1.1–14*
Two actors stand centrally – perhaps with gift tags tied round their necks.

Present 1	So when are they going to open us then?
Present 2	Well, if it's anything like last year, they'll wait until after the Queen's speech this afternoon.
Present 1	How do you know that?
Present 2	Oh, didn't I tell you? I've been a present in this house before. I was given a couple of years ago but I wasn't wanted. I was put inside a drawer upstairs and then this year they suddenly remembered that they hadn't got a present for Aunt Bessie. It was too late to go out to the shops to buy anything so they rooted around upstairs and found me.

Present 1	Is Aunt Bessie going to want a packet of men's hankies?
Present 2	I doubt it. All I know is that it's just good to get out of that drawer.
Present 1	Well, it's the thought that counts.
Present 2	And exactly what thought have they put into me?
Present 1	Good point. Still, I'm sure she'll sound very grateful.
Present 2	'Oooh, how lovely. You shouldn't have. They're just what I wanted.' That's what she'll say.
Present 1	Well, that's nice.
Present 2	If she actually meant any of it, it would be. But actually what she'll be thinking is, 'Well! After all the trouble I've gone to getting exactly the right thing for them. This is what they give me. Hankies! And so obviously men's ones as well. I bet they had them tucked away at the back of some drawer upstairs. I don't know why I bother, I really don't.' I'll bet you that's what she thinks.
Present 1	Oh dear, now you've made me all upset . . . and on Christmas Day too.
Present 2	Look, I'm sorry – I didn't mean to. It's just that words really are *just* words. Sometimes people say one thing and mean another.
Present 1	They forget that this entire celebration is about a word.
Present 2	Ah . . . not 'a' word . . . 'THE' Word. Now that's entirely different – none of your weak words of thanks there. None of your saying one thing but meaning something entirely different.
Present 1	Oh no – this Word has power.
Present 2	Power enough to make things happen.
Present 1	To bring things into existence.
Present 2	To create.
Present 1	Give life.
Present 2	What a powerful Word.
Present 1	And the Word comes into creation.
Present 2	Born as one of us.
Present 1	A baby.
Present 2	Weak and helpless.
Present 1	Yet powerful beyond measure.
Present 2	Why can't they see that?
Present 1	I don't know. If they did see how important it was they wouldn't even dream of giving second-rate presents to honour it.
Present 2	No, indeed . . . oh . . . wait a minute . . . here they come. The Queen must have finished. Wish me luck. *(Exits as if being carried away)*
Present 1	Bye. I won't be far behind . . .

First Sunday of Christmas Year A

Isaiah 63.7–9   Hebrews 2.10–18   Matthew 2.13–23

The thank-you letter   *Isaiah 63.7–9*

There should be as strong a contrast between the two letters as possible. The first should be delivered with a heavy sense of sarcasm, the second with deep and profound awe.

Dear Uncle Tony and Aunty Joan,
Thank you so much for the packet of very useful handkerchiefs that you bought me for Christmas this year. You can never have enough hankies, can you? I know that *you* must believe this, because you send them to me so regularly – every Christmas . . . and birthday as well. Aren't I lucky? It really is very kind of you to think of me in this way. I enjoy quite good health most of the time, but if I ever do get a cold, I shall be well provided for, because my drawers are overflowing with your offerings. It was especially kind of you to send me a Thomas the Tank Engine selection of handkerchiefs this year. Now that I am 45, I find that I am enjoying the nostalgia of steam trains more and more. How delightful to be able to blow my nose at a business meeting and see Thomas's smiling face staring back at me. Ruth has also asked me to send on her grateful thanks for the sensible whisk that you gave her. She finds your advice about her cooking so helpful on your occasional visits, and she is thankful for your kindness in drawing her attention to how she can improve in the kitchen.

   We do hope that you have had a lovely Christmas and we are very much looking forward to your eight-day visit with us in January. It cannot come soon enough! With very best wishes,
Geoff

Dear God,
Peaches and waterfalls and early morning mists and rainbows and baby's fingers and snow-covered mountain tops and music and laughter and butterfly wings. I am overwhelmed, dear friend. I cannot thank you enough for the amazing, joy-filled, wonderful things that surround me every day. Your kindness to me, dear God: it overwhelms me – I cannot even begin to grope for words that are adequate to express how I feel. But it is not enough that you have given me a world that contains tigers and dolphins and ants and oceans. It is not enough that you surround me with skies covered in glittering stars. No – none of this is enough for you. In

your infinite kindness – in your love for me – you have made it possible for me to understand and feel love, and you have shown your grace to me by sharing your love with me at Christmas.

For your kindness to me, Lord, which I can never repay, I will spend the rest of my days in humble thanks.

Thank you, Lord.

With love,

Jenny

Lamberton and Phipps on ways of working   *Hebrews 2.10–18*

Lamberton is landed gentry and very posh; Phipps is his butler. Both are standing centrally. Phipps is long-suffering and far wiser than his master. Costumes could be worn but are not necessary.

Lamberton	I say, Phipps, old man, I have a bit of a question to ask you.
Phipps	You do, sir?
Lamberton	Yes . . . strangest thing is, I'm not sure how to word it. You would have thought that a dashed expensive education at St Oswald's Academy for the Permanently Posh would have stood me in better stead.
Phipps	Indeed, sir.
Lamberton	Look, it's like this . . . what I would like to know is . . . oh dash it all!
Phipps	Sir?
Lamberton	Do you enjoy working for me? There . . . I've said it.
Phipps	Do I enjoy working for you, sir?
Lamberton	Well, don't just repeat the question, hang it all, Phipps. Look. I was having a bit of a chinwag with one of my old school chums, 'Basher' Harris, the other day. And while we were reminiscing about old times, he said the most extraordinary thing. He said that servants should enjoy working for their employers, that it should be a relationship of loyalty and even love. I told him to go and make an appointment at the doctor's. But you know, Phipps, I can't get what he said out of my mind.
Phipps	Is that so, sir?
Lamberton	It is so, Phipps, it jolly well is. You've been my butler now for years.
Phipps	I have indeed, sir.

Lamberton	You've been my constant companion, you have picked me up and given me a good shake when I've been down, you've rescued me from more sticky situations than I can even begin to remember. We have had many a grand jape together.
Phipps	Quite so, sir.
Lamberton	Well, some working relationships are based on fear, some are based on what you can get out of it. I was hoping that ours was based on something a bit more solid than that.
Phipps	Can I speak candidly, sir?
Lamberton	Always welcome candid thought, Phipps, old man.
Phipps	You could make me serve you, sir. You could order me to serve you. I could serve you out of guilt or out of fear. In actual fact, none of those are true. I serve you, sir, because I want to and because in that service I find the freedom to be who I was meant to be.
Lamberton	Gosh, Phipps, I . . . I'm welling up inside.
Phipps	*(Clearing his throat)* Let us never speak of this again, sir.
Lamberton	Quite so, Phipps, quite so. Bad form . . . never again. But, Phipps?
Phipps	Yes, sir?
Lamberton	Thank you.

Power and fear   *Matthew 2.13–23*
This meditation needs to be delivered with restraint but deep feeling.

It is a story that is echoed down the ages.

Wherever fear and power come together in their lethal combination, it has the possibility of taking place all over again.

It is, of course, possible to wield power with generosity, kindness, wisdom, love. Too often, though, that is not the case.

Too often the love of power becomes everything, and those who hold it would do anything – literally anything – to hold on to it.

And so it happens again and again.

There are petty dictators, generals and presidents, who are terrified of asking the voters what they really think.

There are leaders who twist the information their people see and hear, so that only official versions are ever encountered.

There are the power-hungry, who make sure that come election time no real choice is to be had.

The fatal combination of power and fear makes people do the most terrible things. Populations are massacred, children are murdered, freedom is a distant dream.
For there are those who will do anything – literally anything – to hold on to the power they have, even though their power is an illusion, and small and of little importance.
And God . . . who has always been more interested in the powerless than those who think they have power . . . weeps tears of hot anger.

First Sunday of Christmas Year B

Isaiah 61.10—62.3   Galatians 4.4–7   Luke 2.22–40

Meditation   *Isaiah 61.10—62.3*
This meditative thought on the Isaiah verses can be delivered as a straight reading.

'Results that can be observed – that's what I want to see', said the inspector with the air of somebody who believes with all her heart that she is right.
'It might not be as simple as that', I thought to myself. It's not always that easy.
Or is it?
I actually believe that if something of real importance, of life-changing significance, has taken place, then perhaps you ought to be able to see the results.
Perhaps they should grow up naturally – as a plant breaks through the surface of the soil.
I mean – if something really important has taken place, surely you ought to be able to tell?
If we knew – really knew that God's salvation was true for us – then surely things would be different?
Surely the world would ring out with joy, surely righteousness and justice would blossom and grow and burst out everywhere?
Surely we would find it the most difficult thing in the world to sit by while oppression took place or poor people suffered?
Surely all the world would know of our anger at injustice and violence and war?
Surely irrepressible joy would bubble up in everything that we touched or spoke about?

Surely?

As the words of the prophet tumble out in unexpected excitement and joy . . .

Surely the same should be true of us?

And if that is not true . . . not the case . . .

Then perhaps, just perhaps, the challenge lies with us.

'Results that can be observed – that's what I want to see.'

The idea   *Galatians 4.4–7*

A bank manager is sitting centrally. Gerald should be dressed with an eye for eccentricity – slightly unkempt and wild-looking.

Wesley	Send in my next appointment please.

Enter Gerald – he is rather eccentric

Gerald	Ah, yes, good morning, Mr Cutter.
Wesley	Mr Walker, isn't it?
Gerald	Yes, it is, yes.
Wesley	So what can we at First Alliance Bank do for you today, Mr Walker?
Gerald	I have a business proposition for you, Mr Cutter – a rare and wonderful opportunity for you to make loads and loads of money – and I know as a bank that is what you like doing most of all.
Wesley	Well, we're all about listening to our customers and helping them achieve their dreams actually, Mr Walker.
Gerald	While making huge amounts of money in the bargain.
Wesley	Indeed yes.
Gerald	Well, I was sitting in my garden shed the other day thinking to myself, and I thought – 'What is it that most people want?'
Wesley	Goodness – I just think about compost when I'm in the shed. And did you come up with an answer?
Gerald	Well, actually, yes, I did. Yes.
Wesley	*(Pause)* And the answer was?
Gerald	Oh, yes, sorry. Just pausing for dramatic effect. The answer is that people want to feel that they belong. They want a sense of identity – they want to feel accepted and loved.
Wesley	And you've worked out a way of making money from this deep need within people?

Gerald	I have indeed. I'm going to launch a magazine called 'Belong?' – the question mark is very important – it makes people doubt themselves and thus want to buy the magazine to find out whether they do belong or not. It will have all kinds of articles with coloured photographs and graphs and things.
Wesley	Well, it is true that many people have a deep sense of insecurity and a need to find their place in the world.
Gerald	They certainly do, and I intend to make much money out of it.
Wesley	I mean we wouldn't want them realizing the fact that they've been adopted as sons and daughters by the great and mighty God who created the stars and the heavens now, would we?
Gerald	Well, that would mean they'd find their identity and sense of belonging, wouldn't it? So 'no', that would be a very bad thing.
Wesley	*(Long pause)* Mr Walker, I think we can make a great deal of money together.
Gerald	I thought you might say that.

New Testament news   *Luke 2.22–40*

Aaron Hardhitter, a slightly pompous, self-important newsreader is sitting at his desk. A suitable piece of newsroom theme music could be played as an introduction.

Good evening, I am Aaron Hardhitter, and this is the New Testament News. This just in – there was quite a scene in the temple today as two feisty pensioners made their presence felt. Most of us, when we get to our eighties, might be content to sit back, watch the world go by and collect our pension – but that's not the case for outspoken prophetess, Anna. She's been a regular fixture at the Temple for years now – praying and fasting and generally being holy day and night. The same could also be said of Simeon, another tough old character who has been a fixture down in the holy precincts for almost as long as Anna. Well, today was no ordinary day as both of these fiery old folks suddenly started singing, shouting out and generally causing a commotion. Simeon started crying out about being given permission to die, and Anna started pulling aside anybody who would listen to tell them about the redemption of Jerusalem. Ruth Jacobson who was just visiting the Temple from Capernaum said, 'It was very distressing, I thought the Temple was meant to be a place of quiet contemplation – I wasn't expecting anything quite so raucous.' Seth Cohen, spokesperson for the Temple authorities, informed us this afternoon that the Temple would not be seeking to take any further action against these two cantankerous characters and tried to make light of today's disturbances, saying that it provided an interesting half-hour of excitement to a small crowd of bystanders who had gathered. And the cause of all of this fuss? Well, reports are a little confused on this point, but the focus of Simeon and Anna's excitement would appear to be a young couple bringing their child for his purification ceremony. Joseph and Mary, who hail from Nazareth, were not available for comment and seemed to have slipped quietly away in all the commotion. Why this couple caused this kind of excitement in these two holy pensioners is unknown at this point, but the speculation is that Simeon and Anna seem to have been more interested in the child of Mary and Joseph than they were in the new parents themselves. And the name of the child? Jesus. Exactly what was going on down at the Temple this morning, and does it have any significance? We will probably never know. And now . . . on to the weather.

First Sunday of Christmas Year C

1 Samuel 2.18–20, 26   Colossians 3.12–17   Luke 2.41–52

Growing up   *1 Samuel 2.18–20, 26*
Aaron, a slightly pompous newsreader, is sitting at a newsdesk. A suitable piece of newsroom theme music could be played as introduction.

Aaron   I'm Aaron Hardhitter, and this is the Old Testament News. This just in – a boy called Samuel is growing up to please God under the watchful eye of Eli in the Temple. Now that may not seem like a very newsworthy story to you. 'Where is the latest plague coming from?' you may ask. 'What about floods or walls collapsing simply by the blast of a trumpet? A boy growing up in the Temple is hardly news.' To that we here at Old Testament News would say, 'You could not be more wrong.' Growing up in a way that is pleasing to God and to other people is no mean feat in itself. Eli's sons certainly haven't managed to achieve it. As our recent hard-hitting expose 'Take the

Money and Run' showed, they are just involved in religion for their own benefit – to gain as much money and power as they can. To them, we here at Old Testament News say, 'Shame on you.'

So the fact that Samuel is growing up in a way that is pleasing to God and the people is a pretty big success story. We do like to bring you the occasional 'good news' story on our programme. It would be too easy to fill these bulletins with stories of armies being crushed, kings being murdered, plagues of frogs or the threatened destruction of all humanity. It's good once in a while, therefore, to bring to your attention a story that is full of hope and promise. We know that growing up in today's world can be tough on a young person. Temptations surround the young in ways they have never done before. It has become harder and harder for young people to make good choices and for parents to feel that they are doing the right thing. So we here at Old Testament News thought that it would be good to lead our news bulletin tonight with a story of a young man who is making all the right decisions and who seems to have a bright future ahead of him. Growing up is difficult enough, and to do it well, is impressive. And so to Samuel and Eli we here at Old Testament News would like to send a big 'well done'. You've given us all something to be hopeful about. What you are doing could not be more important.

And in other news, 16 people were injured in a multi-camel pile-up on the Jericho Road earlier on today . . .

Meditation   *Colossians 3.12–17*
This simple meditative poem should be delivered in as simple a way as possible.

Compassion
Kindness
Humility
Gentleness
Patience
Tolerance
Forgiveness
Love
It is quite a list, dear friend.
Do you expect this of us all the time?

All of them?
I can manage some of them,
Some of the time.
But then something will happen and I lose my patience.
I can hear words coming out of my mouth that are hasty,
Unkind, or brusque.
I do something which shows a lack of love.
I bear grudges and am too slow to forgive.
I am not as kind as I would like to be.
I have little or no patience.
Do I really sound as if I am somebody
You would want to work with?
More like a hopeless case.
I need help, dear friend.
I need your help . . . now.
I could never do it by myself.
But I want to.
I want to be all of these things.
I do want to be more of the person that you long for me to be.
I want to fulfil the promise that you placed in me.
So come, come and give me the strength and wisdom and patience
That I will need to be lost in your love.

Who is he?   *Luke 2.41–52*

*Joanna and Ruth are sitting centrally. They are both warm, talkative characters. No
special costuming or effects are needed. They could enter talking from the back.*

Joanna	So have you heard?
Ruth	Heard? Heard what? Come on, if there's some juicy gossip to be told I need to be the first to know.
Joanna	Mary and Joseph got back last night with Jesus.
Ruth	Last night? But that's four days, isn't it? Four days after the rest of us.
Joanna	Well, I heard from Rebecca that it took them a day to get back to Jerusalem, and then they were searching for three days before they found him.
Ruth	Searching for three days? Why in heaven did it take so long? Where on earth did they find him? Down some darkened alley somewhere?

Joanna	No – the reason it took so long was that they found him in the last place you'd ever look for a twelve-year-old boy.
Ruth	Well, don't keep me in suspense. Where was he?
Joanna	They found him . . .
Ruth	Yes? Yes?
Joanna	In the Temple.
Ruth	No!
Joanna	Yes. I can't get my Nathan to synagogue, unless I drag him there myself, but Jesus had been in the Temple for three days solid – and not just listening to the wisdom of leaders of the Temple – oh no. From what I heard, when Mary and Joseph got there, Jesus was sitting there discussing the finer points of theology with the wise men.
Ruth	I told you. Have I not told you before that there is something wrong with that boy?
Joanna	What twelve-year-old in his right mind sits for three days doing anything – yet alone discussing religion with a bunch of old men?
Ruth	It's very strange . . . don't you think?
Joanna	Indeed, it is. I mean, he's a nice enough boy.
Ruth	Oh, lovely, kind, cheerful, but . . .
Joanna	Sometimes he looks at you . . .
Ruth	And it's as if he sees straight inside you.
Joanna	And let's not forget the scandal of the birth.
Ruth	Indeed not.
Joanna	I tell you, that Jesus will bear careful watching.
Ruth	Careful watching indeed. I can't shake the feeling that there's something going on under our very noses.
Joanna	But what? And what about his father?

Second Sunday of Christmas Year A

Jeremiah 31.7–14   Ephesians 1.3–14   John 1.(1–9) 10–18

***Action Time* on being rescued**   *Jeremiah 31.7–14*
Action Time *is a children's TV show presented by the ever enthusiastic Jane. Bob is sitting alongside her as the guest of today's show.*

Jane	Hello everybody, and welcome to *Action Time*! I'm Jane. And on the show this week we're going to talk to a very special person indeed. This is Bob Andrews from the Scarborough Coast Guard station at Bridlington.
Bob	Hello!
Jane	Now, Bob, you had to rescue someone this week that we all know very well, didn't you?
Bob	I'm afraid I did, Jane, yes.
Jane	And who was that silly-billy, Bob?
Bob	Well, Jane, I'm afraid it was your co-presenter Chris together with an entire film crew.
Jane	Now tell me, Bob, why did Chris need rescuing?
Bob	Well, Jane, Chris had been doing a piece of filming on a beach on the east coast. I'm afraid the one thing he hadn't done was to check the tide timetables, so he and his sound and camera operator got cut off, and we had to rescue them.
Jane	In fact, Bob, you had to winch them to safety at some personal risk to yourself, isn't that right?
Bob	Well, the sea can be very dangerous, Jane, and you have to take all the proper precautions. You can't afford to be complacent.
Jane	And complacent is a good word to describe the actions of Chris and the *Action Time* film crew, isn't it, Bob?
Bob	Oh, well, I'm not sure I'd go that far.
Jane	Oh, I would, Bob, I would. In fact I'm quite frankly amazed that you would go out, at some risk to yourself, to rescue such a bunch of unprepared, self-absorbed, big-heads. Tell me, Bob – why do you do it?
Bob	Well, the fact is, Jane, that we promise to. When you're a member of the Coast Guard or a Life Boat crew, you have to promise to help rescue people when they are in danger, and that's what you do.
Jane	Even though the people that you're rescuing clearly don't deserve it?
Bob	Even then.
Jane	Even though the people you rescue could do nothing to be worthy of it?
Bob	We have made a promise that we will try our best to rescue people, and that's what we do.
Jane	The people you rescue must be incredibly grateful to you, Bob.

Bob	Well, Jane, I can tell you that your colleague Chris certainly is. He could hardly stop telling us how happy he was to be rescued, and I'm glad to say he'll be out of hospital soon.
Jane	Great, Bob, just great, and if you're watching, Chris – get better soon. Well . . . being rescued . . . what an amazing and possibly life-changing experience. We'll see you again soon on . . . *Action Time*!

Family   *Ephesians 1.3–14*
This meditative thought on family is addressed to God but should be delivered simply and with feeling.

When you think about it – and I am pretty certain that we don't think about it nearly as much as we ought to, dear friend – it is an absolutely extraordinary idea. It is really quite ridiculous in a lovely, world-changing, beautiful kind of way.

We are close enough to you – our relationship to you is intimate enough for you to make us members of *your* family. We are *your* children. That is quite the most amazing claim to make.

How do you even begin to imagine something *that* immense, that world-changing. We are your children. We have a family relationship with you. You who made stars and DNA and hummingbirds, you who created cliff faces and roaring oceans and caterpillars – you make us your children.

I suppose the idea that really astounds me more than any of the others is that anyone of us can have a personal relationship with you. I can feel you close, I can talk to you, I can rest in your presence. That, to me, is the most wonderful, entrancing, extraordinary idea of all. You come to us, you make us your children you even send us Jesus to make that relationship of close adoptive love possible. I will spend the rest of my life exploring what that means for me and for others. I will long for other people to discover that relationship of deep love for themselves. I will forever be thankful and praise the fact that you have made it possible for me and for everyone.

Thank you . . . dearest friend.

Temporary tents   *John 1.(1–9) 10–18*
The actors enter holding Bibles, discussing with each other. No special costuming is needed.

One	Ladies and Gentlemen, good morning.
Two	Good morning indeed. Today we have something really important to share with you.

One	Indeed we do. John Chapter 1 verse 14 reads 'The Word became human and lived among us.'
Two	Well, it kind of says that . . .
One	Indeed . . . kind of . . .
Two	The Greek words actually say, 'he pitched his tent' among us.
One	Now isn't that a wonderful picture?
Two	God pitches a tent among us.
One	God didn't build a palace among us.
Two	God didn't construct a mighty cathedral in our midst.
One	No . . . God pitched a tent.
Two	I love tents.
One	We're not going to get all nostalgic about your camping days are we?
Two	No, it's just that tents are open to the elements.
One	They are mobile.
Two	And perhaps most important of all – they are temporary.
One	They encourage openness and sharing.
Two	They are inviting and hospitable.
One	And they are temporary.
Two	There's that word again.
One	Temporary.
Two	Right here at the beginning of John's story about Jesus it is absolutely clear that Jesus knew he was a visitor.
One	That he wasn't here for a long time.
Two	Just a short stay.
One	Just a few years.
Two	Around 33 of them.
One	Which isn't very long at all . . .
Two	When you've got to change the world.
One	And in fact his active ministry was a great deal shorter than that.
Two	About three years.
One	And yet in that time he gathered disciples.
Two	He taught . . .
One	He preached . . .
Two	He healed . . .
One	He performed wonders . . .
Two	He confronted and challenged . . .
One	He cared and showed great love . . .
Two	He made powerful people very angry . . .

One	He was tried on trumped-up charges . . .
Two	He was killed . . .
One	And he lived . . .
Two	A temporary tent . . .
One	Pitched among us.
Two	God in the midst of us . . .
One and Two	Amen.

Second Sunday of Christmas Year B

Jeremiah 31.7–14   Ephesians 1.3–14   John 1.(1–9) 10–18

Rescue   *Jeremiah 31.7–14*
This monologue is the voice of someone who has been rescued trying to put how it feels into a letter. It should be delivered simply and with feeling. A prop letter can be used.

Dear Philip,
You know I thought, with an intervening space of 20 years or so, it would become easier to put into words how it feels to be rescued. I suppose I thought that all that time would give me some sense of perspective, some ability to grasp hold of the heart of the experience and express it. I find I have this overwhelming desire to explain to people what it was like – first the experience of needing to be rescued in the first place. I found I constantly went over in my mind the events that led up to it and I couldn't help asking myself the question: Was there anything I could have done or seen that would have prevented the situation? Did I somehow bring it on myself? Was I the author of my own fate? I don't think I'll ever have an answer that fully satisfies me. And then there was the captivity itself. I find I can't put into words how monstrous it feels, how completely powerless I became. The smallest details in a day took on a huge significance simply because those were the only things that I had any control over at all. This sounds stupid now, but I found myself becoming completely obsessed by mealtimes. The time when I prepared food became almost a holy ritual because it was about the only thing that I could decide and act on. And then there was the completely indescribable joy of being rescued. It won't surprise you to know that I was scared witless at first – I was giddy with the possibilities at one moment and numb with the vastness of it at the next. To have the whole of life transformed for you, just like that . . . well, I still find it almost impossible to fit words around it. I am forever humbled to have had

the experience. To know that you need to be rescued and then actually to have it happen . . . well, I will forever (and I mean this) . . . forever be grateful.

The interview   *Ephesians 1.3–14*

Two actors are sitting in a TV-studio interview situation. It is a late-night 'talking heads' show. The Professor is academic and slightly flustered. The difference between the smart interviewer and the shambling professor can be emphasized by costume.

Interviewer	Good evening, we're here tonight at midnight on BBC4 to talk with Professor Walter Kranski about theology. Good evening, Professor.
Professor	Good evening.
Interviewer	Perhaps we could start with an easy question . . . what is theology?
Professor	Ah, well, that is perhaps the most profound and difficult question of all.
Interviewer	Oh dear, I thought we'd started with an easy one.
Professor	I'm afraid not. How we define theology ultimately effects how we define life, death, reason and being. It resonates with the deepest profundities of the universe.
Interviewer	It does what? Never mind . . . don't answer that. But it is exciting, isn't it?
Professor	Well, I don't know about that. As Hans Küng once said . . .
Interviewer	No, no, no, Professor. Don't quote anybody else. Tell me yourself . . . is theology exciting?
Professor	Well I . . .
Interviewer	I mean it should be, shouldn't it? God talk? It should be the most meaningful, exciting, joy-giving, hope-creating thing around.
Professor	Well, if you say so.
Interviewer	I do say so. And I'm afraid, Professor, you've made it boring.
Professor	Well, I object to that.
Interviewer	I'm sure you do . . . but it's true. Why else do you think we're going out at midnight on BBC4? Nobody's interested – and they should be. I mean actually, Professor, you must be really talented.
Professor	Oh . . . am I?
Interviewer	Absolutely – it must take real talent to take the most life-changing, hope-filled, joy-charged event in the whole of the universe and make it boring. I mean how do you manage something like that? It must take real skill.
Professor	Well, I suppose it does really.

Interviewer   That wasn't a compliment. Theology should be the most exciting thing in the world to talk about – and somehow we've got to remember that and recapture some of our amazement and wonder. So from Professor Kranski and myself . . . goodnight.

Monologue   *John 1.(1–9) 10–18*
To be delivered in the style of the voice-over for a documentary – the style of David Attenborough works well.

Throughout history and all over the world one thing has always been at the heart of all human activity. One quest has taken up the waking hours of literally billions of people. Men and women have travelled hundreds, if not thousands, of miles. They have scaled great mountains, forged thundering rivers, taken all kinds of immense risks to search out the answer to the question that has plagued us since the day of our birth. The question is . . . Where is God? Humanity has always had this quest at the centre of its life. Men and women have searched high and low for the answer. They have travelled huge distances to sit at the feet of holy men, they have made great pilgrimages to visit places where they have felt God may be found, they have spent years painstakingly working through the knowledge contained in vast and ancient libraries to discover where spiritual truth may dwell. We have searched diligently for religious enlightenment. We have looked for answers wherever we thought they may be found. We have devoured books that claimed to tell us the truth, visited spiritualists, spent fortunes on those who claimed they could point us towards the truth. We have left no stone unturned. But in all this frantic searching there is one thing that humanity often forgets – and it is this: if we look at the early verses of John's Gospel, a key part of Christian scripture, if we read carefully the words we find there, we discover to our astonishment that in fact, instead of our searching for God, the amazing truth is that God is searching for us. Imagine it if you will: after all that soul-searching, after all those ideas tested and found wanting, after all of that inner anxiety and turmoil – the simple fact is that God may well have come searching for us and we did not even realize it. For is it not the case that the message that Christmas brings us is of a God who is born into the world in the form of a tiny baby? A God who comes specifically and deliberately to make direct contact with us – to show us what God's life might be like and to make it possible for us to enter into relationship with the creator of all that is?

Is it not a little disconcerting to realize that after all that searching, the answer may have been there all the time? But is it not also amazing and humbling to know that the God who creates all there is cares for us so much that nothing is left to chance . . . the search is over . . . love is found?

Second Sunday of Christmas Year C

Jeremiah 31.7–14   Ephesians 1.3–14   John 1.(1–9) 10–18

The truth remains   *Jeremiah 31.7–14*
This simple two-narrator piece needs to be delivered briskly and with feeling. No special costuming or effects are needed.

One	So, the fuss is nearly over.
Two	The presents have been opened.
One	The tree is shedding its needles.
Two	The turkey is nearly finished.
One	The sales are in full swing.
Two	And for some people Christmas is done for another year.
One	Unless it meant more than presents and cards.
Two	Unless overindulgence wasn't the point.
One	There is a truth that remains after the tinsel has been boxed up.
Two	There is meaning after the New Year has begun.
One	If what Christmas celebrates has anything to say at all – it says this . . .
Two	There is a relationship that is possible for each and every one of us.
One	It is a relationship of love.
Two	Not hearts and flowers, romantic indulgence . . .
One	But a love that is sacrificial . . . that comes at immense cost.
Two	And even when you feel far away from home.
One	Even on those occasions when you look at yourself and do not even recognize your own actions, they are so different from the person you thought you were . . .
Two	Even at those times this love supports you and holds you and will not let you go.
One	And this love longs for the good.
Two	And this love comes to take you home.
One	When you are lost, and lonely and so afraid that it hurts . . .
Two	This love rescues you.

One	This love is God.
Two	And people sneer at that . . . and people count it as nothing.
One	They cannot or will not believe.
Two	But God still loves them.
One	And God still longs to bring them home.
Two	And this truth remains.
One	After the tinsel is safely boxed up for another year.
Two	The cards are taken down . . .
One	The food is finished . . .
Two	God's saving, rescuing, sacrificial love remains.
One	And it longs for us to discover it . . .
Two	For ourselves.

Joining in the dance   *Ephesians 1.3–14*

This heartfelt piece on my inability to dance should be delivered with feeling.

You know Lord –
I would love to be able to dance.
I really would.
Graceful and elegant, soaring and natural.
But there is a problem.
I have no grace, and I am rather clumsy.
I am afraid that I would not look elegant – not at all.
I would stumble around and fall.
Heaven forbid that anybody else should have to dance with me.
I would never be at the right place at the right time.
Their arms would reach up and there would be no one to hold.
They would turn round expecting space and I would be there.
Ready to be bumped into.
I would love to be able to take part . . .
But I cannot.
And yet you have called me to dance.
To take part in the music of your creation.
And it doesn't matter how uncoordinated I am.
I will trip and fall many times and you do not mind.
Your dance weaves in and out of my life –
Surrounding me with the colours of your love.
And the most wonderful thing happens.

Even though I am not graceful and have no natural skill,
Simply by being caught up in the choreography of your love
I become beautiful and I soar.
I become part of the story.
I find I have a role to play and it is vital –
As I am swept up in your grace and joy.
I would love to be able to dance.
I really would.
And to my complete and utter amazement
I find that I have a role to play
In the dance of love that weaves creation together.
Thank you.

Not recognized   *John 1.(1–9) 10–18*

This is written from the point of view of somebody who grew up with Jesus and is asking themself why they didn't recognize what was going on. It should be delivered with feeling.

If you were to ask now why I didn't recognize him, I'm not sure I'd be able to tell you. And yes I know how unbelievable that sounds. After all, I grew up in the same town as him. I played with him when he was small.

I was around when his ministry started. We heard the stories – they made their way back to Nazareth. It wasn't so much a case of 'local boy made good' as 'we had no idea'. People were politely interested. They'd occasionally ask Mary questions about what Jesus was up to now, but there was no real connection. It all sounded a little bit remote from our experience. Somehow it didn't tally with what we knew about him. Stories of healings and wonders and a teacher who was so inspirational that crowds followed him . . . we never quite understood. It may have been because we knew him, of course. It's always a bit embarrassing to think that others have seen something you haven't. Somehow I felt that because we'd been around him for so long, knew him so well, we should have recognized it – spotted it – whatever 'it' was. It was a bit odd to think that others had spotted in a very brief time something we'd had under our very noses for years and hadn't seen. But again that familiarity might have been the very reason why we didn't see – didn't understand.

You'd hear the most amazing things. Stories of blind people seeing, deaf people hearing, lepers cleansed. You'd hear stories of mass preaching events, of crowds hanging on his every word, and you'd ask yourself: Do I recognize this person? Is this the same ten-year-old that I hung around with?

It's always the same, isn't it? At least – it is with me. Why don't we recognize really important stuff that's right in front of us? Why don't we spot the person who's been hurt by something we've said? Why don't we recognize the signs that somebody loves us even though they've been sending out all the right signals? Why don't we recognize the huge signpost from God that's right in the middle of our lives?

When I heard about the way he'd died I was shocked again. It didn't seem right . . . crucifixion? Impossible . . . not Jesus. I thought about him a lot after that. The memories I had of growing up. The stories that I'd heard later . . . and the one occasion when I'd heard him speak to a crowd. It was extraordinary. You know, when you hear most people speak it's just a series of words tumbling out one after another. With Jesus it was as if all of those words came together into one meaning, one truth. Rather than lots of little words it was as if he'd spoken one word that gathered all the others up into itself. The word was 'love'. It summed up his actions, his being, his speech – everything about him – one word – love.

To my eternal shame I didn't drop everything right there and then and follow him. But I did later. I recognized who he was – a little late perhaps but I did see it in the end.

Light, love, truth . . . the Word of God . . . right here.

4

Epiphany

The Epiphany

Isaiah 60.1–6   Ephesians 3.1–12   Matthew 2.1–12

Journey to light   *Isaiah 60.1–6*
This two-narrator piece based on the thoughts in Isaiah 60 contains slightly abstract ideas and should be delivered at slightly slower pace.

One	It is hard for words to describe it.
Two	The deep, deep relief.
One	The overwhelming excitement.
Two	The waves of emotion . . .
One	Of hope and joy.
Two	All that happens when you've been in darkness for a long, long time . . .
One	And suddenly you see light.
Two	Perhaps you had lost all hope.
One	Maybe you felt the darkness would last forever.
Two	That nothing or no one could take it away.
One	And then you spot it.
Two	It may be very small at first.
One	So tiny you can hardly see it.
Two	You may not even be convinced that it's there at all.
One	Squinting . . . peering . . . to be certain.
Two	But there it is and unmistakably it's getting larger.
One	Light . . . shedding warmth and understanding.
Two	Brighter and brighter, bathing you in its glow.
One	Illuminating every dark place where shadows cling on.

Two	And then there comes the moment when it washes all over you.
One	And life is transformed.
Two	Everything changes.
One	You can see.
Two	An explosion of colour and life and vitality.
One	New possibilities suddenly emerge.
Two	You can suddenly see what was there all the time.
One	And things begin to make sense.
Two	You want to dance . . .
One	To laugh . . .
Two	To cry . . .
One	But most of all to praise.
Two	To praise with all of your heart and strength . . .
One	The one who has made this possible.
Two	And brought you home.

The secret   *Ephesians 3.1–12*

This exploration of Ephesians 3 is a straight meditative reading and should be delivered as such.

It's just as well, dear friend, that here, in Ephesians, we have an open secret. One that's already been shared, split wide open.

It is just as well that's the case, because I'm not sure I'd be able to keep it if I knew.

I'm actually not bad at keeping secrets . . . I know when to hold my peace . . . not share things that aren't mine to share.

Give me a secret, and it's normally safe . . . especially when it's about something important.

But I'm not sure I could have kept this secret, Lord.

I'm not sure I could kept this news to myself . . . it is too important, too life-changing . . . too good to be kept to yourself.

I couldn't have done it.

I would have wanted to climb to the top of some bell-tower somewhere . . . with a view of miles around,

I would have wanted to clamber to the top of a large hill or mountain peak and shout it . . . proclaim it . . . cry it out into space so that as many could hear it as possible.

As I say, dear, friend, it is just as well this isn't a secret any more
. . . because I couldn't have kept it.
And the secret?
This good news that is so hard to keep?
It's that your love is for everyone.
Absolutely everyone.
Not just for one particular group.
Not just for one part of humanity.
Not only for the people who are like me . . .
Not even for the people that I like or choose . . .
It's for EVERYONE.
And I assume that means it's for the people whom I don't like very much.
The ones I normally try and avoid, cross the street to miss.
It's for them . . . all of them.
Every language, every colour, every race and background.
EVERYONE.
And that is good news, dear friend.
VERY good news.
And I'm so glad that that gift is not a secret! Because I want you to help me in shouting it from the rooftops.

Signs   *Matthew 2.1–12*

This first-person monologue from a member of Herod's court should be delivered in a conversational tone. No special costuming or props are necessary.

It's never been easy. I will tell you that right now. In fact saying 'it isn't easy' is the understatement of the year. That is like saying camels are bad tempered, or that in the summer it gets hot. None of those statements really does justice to the way things are. It has never been easy working for Herod – that's the understatement. The man is a nightmare – violent, completely unpredictable, prone to the most terrible tempers. To work for him is to live in constant fear of your life. You know that every morning when you wake up, the tiniest slip of the tongue, the smallest mistake could see you dead. And the scary thing is that actually you don't have to have done anything wrong at all for him to take against you. It could be as simple as being in the wrong place at the wrong time.

I know what you're thinking: If it is so bad working for him, why don't I leave? Believe me, if I could I would. But he would hunt me down, have me killed in my sleep. The situation is hopeless. My only chance is to outlive him.

But, of course, you don't want to know about my personal problems – they are for me to deal with. You want to know about the visit of the Magi. What a day that was. Of course, we get visitors at the palace all the time. Foreign dignitaries, wealthy important people, Roman bureaucrats – they all come. But that day was different. They arrived from the east, and it was obvious they had journeyed some way. By their dress it was clear they were well off, they had servants with them – a slight whiff of the exotic. We were, initially, all interested to see what was going on. They clearly had a purpose – it was all very exciting.

They were ushered into the royal presence – and even Herod himself leaned forward in his throne – a little more interested than he often is at these sorts of visits. They bowed low before the throne and then came the question that changed everything . . . 'Where is the baby born to be the King of the Jews?' they asked. 'We saw his star when it came up in the east and we've come to worship him.' There was the most deathly silence for what seemed like hours but which, I am assured, was only a few moments. None us of us dared look at Herod because we knew he was looking at us and nobody wanted to catch his eye.

The visitors were ushered out of the throne room with a slightly hurried air of embarrassment and then the shouting started. What King? What baby? What Star? Why had we not spotted it? Why had we not told him? What use were we if we could not get even this simple task right? Of course, the fact was that we had spotted the star – we were just too frightened to tell him because we knew what it would mean. I think we had hoped that if nobody told him he might never find out. But he did. And his anger was a terrible, primal thing to behold.

When the visitors were given a second audience Herod was all charm. 'Oh but you must,' he kept saying, 'you MUST come back here when you've found him and tell me all. Of course, I too must go and pay my respects.' You could almost see the desperation in his eyes.

Well, they left, and they haven't come back. If a new king has been born I, for one, am overjoyed. Earthly kings are much overrated . . . particularly this one. And I long to see something new, something unexpected, something of God come to bring us hope.

5

Lent

First Sunday in Lent Year A

Genesis 2.15–17; 3.1–7   Romans 5.12–19   Matthew 4.1–11

Choices   *Genesis 2.15–17; 3.1–7*
This dramatic monologue is written specifically so that it can be delivered by either Adam or Eve. No special costuming is necessary.

Of course, I regret the choice I made. Is that what you want to hear? Would that make you feel better? Of course, if I had to choose again, I would choose differently. Choose something else – make some other kind of a decision.

The problem is that when we make choices – good or bad – we don't know what the consequences are going to be. How can we? Some choices look quite small at the time, insignificant. It's only later – when you have the luxury of time to look back and ponder your decisions – it's only then that you realize that you've made the most terrible mistake.

And fancy having only one rule. I mean, is that a recipe for potential disaster or what? Give somebody lots of rules and they may not think about breaking any of them, but give people only one rule – one thing that you tell them that they must not do on any account and . . . well, there's going to be nothing more attractive is there? Like moths to a flame – it's quickly going to be the one thing more than anything else that you are going to want to do. It's like giving somebody a red button with a big sign over the top of it. A sign that says 'Don't touch this button'. Why not? What's going to happen if I touch it? The curiosity alone might kill you.

But there's no point in laying blame now. It was our fault – well, not completely our fault, but . . . we had paradise. That's the heartbreaking thing. We had paradise. You have no idea how beautiful it was, how absolutely breathtakingly stunning. Words can't begin to describe. We were so foolish. Why are we like that? Only one rule – one thing that we were told not to do and we couldn't even follow that simple, straightforward instruction. We thought we knew better – we always think we know better, and look where it's left us. So much for humanity being intelligent. What I miss most is the closeness. Those beautiful, tantalizing conversations that were so innocent, so loving. And it's gone . . . for ever. I'm guessing. God would have to do something pretty incredible to restore what's been destroyed . . . something very special indeed – and why would God want to do that?

Grace   *Romans 5.12–19*
This meditative piece on grace is a straight reading and should be delivered as such.

Think about it, for any length of time . . .
Let your mind wander around the idea.
Explore the nooks and crannies of the thought.
And one thing becomes more and more obvious and overwhelming.
Grace is the most extraordinary thing.
As we think about it, the first thing we try to do is justify ourselves . . .
Surely there must be something we could do to be worthy of it?
Surely there is something we could do to repay the cost?
After all, nobody likes to be in debt.
But that's just the thing . . . we are.
Deeply, deeply in debt.
And there is nothing that we can do.
The separation is too great – the gulf to be crossed too wide.
The solution has to come from God.

We also really do not like the fact that it's free.
We do not trust things that look this good.
'Nothing comes for free' we've been told.
Except this does.
And there is absolutely nothing we can do that would pay the price of it.
Nothing.

What we need to do is open ourselves up to it.
Stop fighting and struggling against it.
Relax into it and allow it to wash over and through us.
Refreshing us, recreating us and leading us where it will.
This is grace – and in every possible way – it is amazing.

Go on   *Matthew 4.1–11*

Rob is standing centrally – Gary enters from behind him and saunters up. Rob is serious and thoughtful, Gary is clearly subtle purest evil. Rob is pondering doing something wrong which is purposely not identified.

Gary	*(Looking over Rob's shoulder)* Well, hello.
Rob	Oh! Ah . . . sorry, you scared me for a minute then. Who are you?
Gary	Well, I'm known by many names actually, but you can call me Gary.
Rob	Hi, I'm Rob.
Gary	I know. Forgive me for saying, but you look troubled, Rob.
Rob	Is it that obvious?
Gary	I'm afraid it is. The furrowed brow, the restless feet – not good signs you know.
Rob	It's just that I've got lot on my mind.
Gary	You don't say. Look, Rob – let's cut to the chase shall we? We both know that you're thinking of doing something ever so naughty. Why don't you just go ahead and do it?
Rob	It is tempting.
Gary	Isn't it just? And think how much better you'll feel when it's done. All these messy emotions that you're currently wrestling with will just go away.
Rob	But it's wrong.
Gary	Wrong? Oh come on, Rob, you're more sophisticated than that. What's right? What's wrong? It's all in the eye of the beholder. They're such relative terms.
Rob	But what if somebody finds out?
Gary	Now please, people only find out in TV soap operas. This is the real world: nobody ever finds out. Go on . . . you know you want to. It's not even that serious a crime . . . you might not even get jail time.
Rob	It would solve a lot of my problems.
Gary	Of course it would – and think of how free you'll feel when it's done.
Rob	But what if something goes wrong?
Gary	Exactly what could go wrong? Come on now, for goodness sake: man-up and do the deed.
Rob	But somebody could get hurt.

Gary	Look, thousands of people get hurt every day – most of the time it's their own fault. So exactly what is the problem?
Rob	You make such good sense.
Gary	It's a gift I possess. I help clouded minds see things a little more clearly.
Rob	And yet I don't know if I should trust you.
Gary	Well, that's your choice, isn't it, Rob? You can trust me . . . honestly. I never lie. *Gary exits.*

First Sunday in Lent Year B

Genesis 9.8–17   Mark 1.9–15

Old Testament News   *Genesis 9.8–17*
Aaron is a slightly pompous newsreader, sitting at a desk. If suitable newsroom theme music can be played, it will add atmosphere.

Aaron	I'm Aaron Hardhitter and this is the Old Testament News. This is just in. Local townspeople watch in amazement as a huge boat is built in their backyard. Stunned disbelief turned into anger this afternoon as residents in the suburbs expressed their pent-up frustration with well-known eccentric Noah. The 600-year-old man together with the rest of his family have been busy over the past few months building a huge boat in the spacious backyard of their pleasant home in a residential area.
	Local housewife Rachel Harris said, 'It's gone too far, we were prepared to put up with a bit of DIY, but this is ridiculous.' Local planning officials were being called in this afternoon to check whether the relevant planning permissions had been applied for. The boat, which is 300 cubits long and 30 cubits high, is becoming something of a tourist attraction.
	People from as far as 20 miles away are coming to see what's been going on in Noah's garden. And we're hearing unconfirmed reports that pest-control officials are also being called in as a strange array of animals appear to be roaming the streets around Noah's home. There is no way of knowing at this time whether the two stories are related although some local sources are sure that they've seen animals entering the boat itself, 'two by two'. Local

animal control warden Snitch Yeardley said, 'If Noah is thinking of turning this boat into some kind of themed animal sanctuary then there are all kinds of regulations he's in breach of.' We were unable to talk to Noah himself as he appeared to be up a ladder putting some finishing touches to this huge construction project, but his son Ham did give us this comment: 'God has told us to do this; you're all going to die because of your sinful ways.' Local residents responded that they were no more sinful than anybody else. And the location of Noah's grand boat? We've been asked by concerned local councillors not to divulge that crucial piece of information, but suffice it to say that it is more than 45 miles away from the nearest sea. At Old Testament 6 News all we can say is that we hope this feisty pensioner knows what he's doing, because the neighbours are getting restless. And now over to Gill Rainey with the weather.

Gill   Well, Aaron, Noah might need that big boat to shelter in, because we've got what looks to be a large area of low pressure coming in from the west. The first rain won't reach us until tomorrow, and I'm confident that it will be fairly light and patchy when it does arrive. There might be occasional heavy showers over the hills, but I think all low-lying areas should escape the worst of the weather. Accompanying the rain, winds will pick up a bit, and it'll feel quite breezy after the early morning mist has cleared. However, I have to say that I'm sure that the weather for the weekend is going to be beautiful, with lots of sunshine.

Aaron   Thanks for that, Gill. Join us tomorrow night as we continue our occasional series on the moral decline of the nation. Crime levels soar, evil escalates, and the authorities seem to be doing nothing. The question we're asking tomorrow is: 'Have people forgotten God?' Be sure to join us then, and in the meantime, this is Aaron Hardhitter and Gill Rainey wishing you a powerful day.

What are we for?   Mark 1.9–15

This stream of thoughts on the purpose of life occasioned by Mark 1 is a non-dramatic meditation and should be delivered as such.

I got a phone call the other day. It came at about half past six. I was just sitting down to eat when the phone rang. Muttering under my breath I picked it up.

I should have known better, I really should, because there's only one kind of phone call I get about half past six. 'This is an important call,' said a pre-recorded voice, 'would you like to consolidate all your debts into one easily repaid loan?' I won't tell you what I said as I put the phone down with rather more force than was needed.

I know what they're trying to do. They're playing on our fear. 'The world is a dark and difficult place,' they're saying, 'and you're in out of your depth.' They want me to believe that they can put me back in control. They want me to think that it is possible to be in charge of my life. That if I just have enough insurance or life coverage or a small enough monthly loan repayment that will take me the next 25 years to clear – if I have all of that then life will be good because I will be in control. Nothing unexpected could possibly happen and even if it does I will have insured myself against every possible eventuality.

They want me to rest easy. They don't want me to think too hard. They want me to conform, to protect myself.

As I step into the journey that Lent represents, I just wonder whether there are some bigger questions that I ought to be asking myself. Not 'Am I safe and protected?' but rather, 'What am I for?', 'What do I depend on?' It's precisely those questions that I'm slightly nervous of. Those big, life-changing, difficult-to-wrestle-with questions, which are important to ask. I don't ask them enough, because I think that what I spend most of my life doing is protecting myself from God. It's ironic (isn't it?) that I spend all that time and energy buying protection and insuring my life in order to protect myself against God.

At the beginning of his ministry Jesus opened himself up to God and all of the possibilities that went along with that. He asked the difficult, heart-searching, purpose-driving questions. Is there a reason — apart from protecting myself from answers that might be unnerving — that I don't do the same?

First Sunday in Lent Year C

Deuteronomy 26.1–11   Luke 4.1–13

Remembering   *Deuteronomy 26.1–11*
This letter should be delivered as if you are reading it direct. A letter as a prop will help.

Dear Julie,
I thought I would just write you a letter. Yes – a handwritten letter on a piece of paper. It will be a long time since you had one of those. Perhaps you've never

received one. I know – I'm sounding like the old dinosaur that I probably am. I also know that you're far more likely to be on Facebook or Skype or Twitter – chatting with your friends in short bursts of language. But in my experience, at least, there is nothing like the excitement of getting a handwritten note dropped onto your mat in the morning post. It means something. It means someone has taken the time to sit down at a desk, find some paper and a pen and write something with you especially in mind. How glorious. They've then found a stamp – gone to a postbox and dropped the thing in the mail. Now that's exciting. I can remember as a child rushing downstairs as soon as I heard the post delivered to see if there was anything for me.

I've been thinking a lot about that recently. Not the post – but remembering. I'm beginning to realize how important it is. It actually forms us. I don't think that you can understand anything about who you are or why things are the way they are without memory. The things we choose to remember and the ways we choose to do that are incredibly important. We surround ourselves with hundreds of little rituals, actions that help us to remember – and those things make us the people that we are.

I know – I'm carrying on like an old fool. And no doubt you'll turn round to me and say these things are all in the past. I've got to face forwards – forget the past – embrace the future. But I don't want remembering to be a stale, dusty thing that stops us moving forward. I want it to be a moving, exciting, dynamic thing that helps us to make the future as wonderful as it should be because we understand how the past has shaped it.

I don't know whether you see the importance of any of this, but to me the past and how we remember it and carry it with us is one of the most important questions we face.

Anyway, Julie – I hope you've enjoyed getting this letter . . . a real 'blast from the past' in itself. Do think about what I've said. What we choose to remember and how we do that are, I think, more important than we know.
Best wishes, Gran

Finding yourself *Luke 4.1–13*

A hotel check-in desk is central. Standing behind it is a member of staff – a customer enters. Both characters should be bright and chatty.

| Clerk | Ah good, morning, good morning. Welcome to the Hotel Grand View. How may I help you? |
| Guest | Well, I was hoping I might check in as a guest here for three or four nights. |

Clerk	Certainly Sir/Madam, certainly. We have a number of excellent room choices available. What kind of accommodation were you looking for?
Guest	Well, I need a room that's going to help me with the job I've got to do.
Clerk	Pardon me – I don't understand.
Guest	Well, I've got a job I want to do over the next few days, and I want a room that's going to get me in the right frame of mind for my work.
Clerk	I see, and exactly what kind of job do you want to do?
Guest	I want to find myself.
Clerk	I'm sorry . . .
Guest	Well, before I start the rest of my life, I just want to take a few days to find myself. Work out who I am, what kind of person I want to be.
Clerk	I see.
Guest	Most people never really work it out – but I want to. I want to make some key choices about the kind of person I'm going to be. For example, am I going to be a patient person, or am I going to have a bit of a temper . . . you know – be a kind of volcano always ready to blow?
Clerk	Goodness me.
Guest	Am I going to be a dishonest person – constantly looking out for ways of cheating other people – or am I going to be essentially honest, known for my integrity and trustworthy nature?
Clerk	I see. And you're going to do all of that over the next three or four days here at our hotel?
Guest	I am – do you have a good room-service menu by the way? I might be eating in a lot.
Clerk	Excellent. May I recommend a room on one of our higher floors with a lovely view of the mountains? It might help you in your work.
Guest	That's the idea.
Clerk	I have to say you're the first person who has made a request of this kind.
Guest	I'm sure I am. Most people kind of drift through life without really thinking too clearly about the kind of person they want to be. They get pushed around by each new event and end up making their decisions off the cuff. I want to be different from that.

Clerk	Don't we all?
Guest	I want to think through the kind of person I'm going to be right now.
Clerk	Admirable.
Guest	So that when difficult times come I'll be ready.
Clerk	Here, here!
Guest	Are you with me?
Clerk	With you? I'm going to check in too! All we have to do is sign in the register here . . . and here.

They exit talking

Second Sunday in Lent Year A

Genesis 12.1–4a   Romans 4.1–5, 13–17   John 3.1–17

The journey   *Genesis 12.1–4a*
This dialogue is set in a travel agents (a suitable sign on a desk might be helpful). Abram walks in . . . no special costuming is necessary, though a desk, chair and phone will be needed.

Travel Agent	*(On the phone)* So, that's two tickets for our all – inclusive bargain break to Joppa . . . lovely *(Covers phone and talks to Abram)* Do take a seat sir, I won't be a moment. *(To phone customer)* Yes, it does include all camel feed. And you'll come in and pick them up next week? Lovely. *(Replaces phone)* Now then Mr . . . ?
Abram	Abram.
TA	Lovely. What can I do for you today?
Abram	Well, this is going to sound rather strange.
TA	Don't you worry . . . you'd be surprised at some of the requests we get at Sunrise Travel. Now where would you like to go?
Abram	I'm not really sure.
TA	Lovely – well, Egypt is nice at this time of year, and we've got some spectacular island packages.
Abram	No, you don't understand. The only reason that I don't know where I'm going yet is because I haven't been told.
TA	Oh . . . the lovely lady not decided where she wants you to take her yet?

Abram	No . . . God hasn't told me yet.
TA	*(Pause)* God?
Abram	Yes – God's told me that I'm to go, but hasn't told me where yet.
TA	You're letting God dictate your holiday plans?
Abram	Well, it's not really a holiday . . . more a journey of discovery.
TA	Lovely. And you don't know where you're going?
Abram	No . . . I've got to pack up everything I own, and then God will show me where I'm going once we get started.
TA	I don't want sound rude . . . but that's awfully trusting of you.
Abram	Yes . . . I suppose it is really. Anyway, I came in here, because I thought you might have some maps you could let me have.
TA	*(Gathering together some maps)* And they could be of . . .
Abram & TA	Anywhere really.
TA	Lovely.
Abram	*(Taking maps)* Well, thank you very much, you've been very kind.
TA	Oh, don't mention it. I hope your journey goes well. Can we offer you any insurance?
Abram	No thank you . . .
TA	Trusting in God . . . I get it.

Deeds, law, faith   *Romans 4.1–5, 13–17*

This meditative poem on Romans 4 should be delivered simply. More than one voice can be used.

I fight so hard to ignore it, Lord.
I fight, because I don't want to hear it.
I don't want to hear that the only thing you need from me is faith.
I don't want to hear that, because it means I've got to hand myself over
to you.
Fully and completely – no strings attached.
I don't like that idea, Lord.
I don't like the lack of control it implies.
I still want to do things my way.
I want to retain some sense of power.
I want to be able to do the occasional good deed,
And think that by doing it I've come closer to you.
I want to be able to point to the deeds of others and

Think that mine are somehow better.

I want to be able to follow laws and instructions.

I want to feel that there is some kind of code I need to stick to.

It means I don't have to look at my walk with you as a relationship –

A relationship that requires trust and understanding and love.

Why did you make it so free, Lord?

Why did you make it about love?

It would be so much easier if there was a rule book to follow.

Then I could keep a level of control.

It would be so much better if I knew that I could rack up good deeds in heaven.

Then I could keep some sort of checklist.

But no.

You want faith.

You want trust.

You want love.

You want nothing less than the whole of me.

Starting now.

Nicodemus remembers   *John 3.1–17*

This first-person monologue delivered by Nicodemus should be informal and conversational. No special costuming is necessary.

I know what you're thinking. Really, I do. There he is . . . Nicodemus, skulking around in the middle of the night. Going to Jesus under the cover of darkness – what a coward. Why not ask your questions in the cold light of day? Why not go openly, publicly and ask what you want to where everybody else can see?

It wasn't like that. Really, it wasn't. Yes I went at night but there wasn't anything underhand about it. I mean I didn't creep around at midnight under a cloak or anything like that. I just couldn't get close during the day. There were always people around, pressing in, chattering about this and that. I just thought I'd go when I was more likely to find Jesus at a quiet moment, by himself. Is that so wrong?

He had only just started his ministry but he was already creating a bit of a stir. And I have to admit I was fascinated. I hadn't gone to trip him up, or put him on the spot. I was genuinely interested in finding out what he had to say. So how do you start a conversation like that? What opening gambit do you use? I decided to tell him how much I admired him and how we all could see that he was a teacher sent from God. Anyone could see that that there was something extraordinary about him.

He looked at me with those eyes. Those eyes that seemed to be seeing so much more than ordinary eyes do. He looked at me and he said the most extraordinary thing. I remember it as if it was yesterday because they were not at all the words that I expected to hear after such a polite and, dare I say it, flattering opening on my part. 'I am telling you the truth,' he said, 'no-one can see the Kingdom of God unless he is born again.' What a way to start a relationship! What was I meant to say to that? I mean at the time I didn't even understand. Not one bit of it. It's taken years of journeying, thinking, reflecting to come even close to working out what went on over the next ten minutes. My mind was stretched like it had never been stretched before. All that I thought I knew was turned on its head. And not in a gentle, 'let's tease this idea out together' kind of a way. No – it was challenging, bombastic, tear-down-the-walls kind of talk.

I came to Jesus and I was welcomed and then my entire life was transformed. But then, when you come to Jesus, anything can happen.

Second Sunday in Lent Year B

Genesis 17.1–7, 15–16   Mark 8.31–8

Trust me   *Genesis 17.1–7, 15–16*
This first-person monologue by Abraham should be delivered with deeply felt conviction. No special costuming or props are necessary.

How can you tell? That's what I'd like to know . . . what I *need* to know. How can you tell when to trust? Particularly when you're being asked to do something so radical, so different from anything that you've done before that you begin to wonder whether there might be something wrong with your hearing.

Okay – look, let's start at the beginning. I'm an old man, right? Not just middle aged . . . old. Bones creak, my sight is not what it used to be. My days of doing wild and crazy things are well behind me. Oh I'll have you know they happened – wild and crazy days. Days when I thought I could do anything . . . take on the world. They definitely are there . . . in the past . . . but not now. Not anymore.

And then came the day . . . that day when God came into my life. Not in a quiet, tip-toeing kind of a way you understand . . . more of a blinding light, crash of thunder kind of a way. I fell on my knees. The intensity – the power . . . I couldn't stand. And God spoke with me. Words flashed like glints of sunlight in my brain and I knew – somehow I knew they were the words of God. Though when I understood the words I could hardly believe they were aimed at me. Somebody else . . . surely? There must have been some kind of a mistake. A covenant . . . with me . . . to start a new nation? This, surely, was God's idea of a joke . . . though I must admit I wasn't laughing. There was even a change of name . . . Abram to Abraham, Sarai to Sarah.

The idea of Sarah and I being some kind of leaders, having children, founding a nation. It seems outrageous, nonsensical. Surely there were easier routes to be taken . . . more obvious choices that could have been made. But no – apparently this is what God wants. And I . . . I have said 'yes'. When God comes knocking at your door, what else can you say? I'm still rather sceptical . . . still not sure I believe or understand what's going on. Which brings me back to the question that I started with. How can you tell when to trust? Don't worry – I'm not expecting you to be able to answer. But the answer is going to come soon enough. And I am going to reach up . . . grasp God's hand and let it lead where it will. What a grand adventure!

Losing and Saving   *Mark 8.31–8*

One and Two walk forward from the back talking as they move in a conversational style. No special costuming or effects are necessary.

One	So one day, Jesus took his disciples to one side and began to teach them.
Two	He was a fantastic teacher, but on this particular day he had a difficult lesson to teach his friends.
One	They found it hard to listen to. He told them that terrible times were coming. He told them that the Son of Man would go through great suffering . . . that the scribes and the elders and the chief priests – all those people who should have been wiser – more open to the ways of God – would reject him.
Two	Not only would they reject him but they would see to it that he was put to death.
One	But three days after that death he would rise.
Two	*(Pause)* He spoke plainly.
One	Perhaps too plainly, because Peter . . .
Two	Who was capable of a bit of plain speaking of his own . . .
One	. . . began to get upset with all of this and told Jesus that this could not be so.

Two	Well, this upset Jesus.
One	Really it did. This was an important lesson that his friends had to hear and understand.
Two	So he turned on Peter and said,
One	'Out of my sight, Satan! You think as humans think, not as God thinks.'
Two	Well, you can imagine how difficult that was for Peter to hear.
One	He was only trying to be protective.
Two	But Jesus didn't need protecting.
One	In fact he carried on speaking as people gathered.
Two	'Anyone who wants to be a follower of mine . . .'
One	He said . . .
Two	'Needs to forget themselves, pick up their cross and follow me.
One	If you want to save your life . . .
Two	You need to lose it.
One	And whoever loses their life for my sake . . .
Two	Will save it!
One	If you win all that the world has to offer . . .
Two	Power, money, fame . . .
One	But it's cost you your life . . .
Two	You've lost.
One	This world is difficult but if you are ashamed of me and the words I speak . . .
Two	Then I'll be ashamed of you when I come back in glory.
One	With my Father and the holy angels.'

Second Sunday in Lent Year C

Genesis 15.1–12, 17–18   Luke 13.31–5

State your case   *Genesis 15.1–12, 17–18*
Two actors stand centrally. One is confident and honest to the point of rudeness, Two is anxious and hesitant. No special costuming or props are necessary.

One	O Lord, I do get angry with you sometimes.
Two	*(Shocked)* Shhh! For goodness sake what on earth are you doing?

One	I'm telling God how I feel – and I feel really angry at the moment.
Two	Angry at your situation I'm sure . . .
One	No, angry at God.
Two	Look – be quiet!
One	What do you mean?
Two	Well, you can't be cross with God. God is . . . well . . . God is . . . just God, that's all. God is all-loving all-glorious, all-powerful. And God is everywhere . . . you know, God could be listening to you right now.
One	Good . . . then he or she will hear me then, won't they?
Two	B-b-but God might get cross with you – and smite you with a plague or a lightning bolt or something. And you know, I'm only standing two feet to the left of you . . . it could hit me instead.
One	But if God is all-loving then God wouldn't smite me with anything.
Two	Well, I don't know . . . it just doesn't feel like a very good idea to make the creator of the universe cross with you, that's all. He . . . or she is rather more powerful than you are.
One	Look – isn't honesty in relationships important?
Two	Well, yes . . .
One	In fact the closer the relationship the more honest you can be . . . isn't that right?
Two	I suppose . . .
One	You don't have to put on any show for them – you can actually be yourself.
Two	Alright.
One	Well then – I'm so close to God that I feel comfortable enough to tell God honestly how I feel. And I feel cross.
Two	Well, just leave me out of it . . . okay?
One	It's okay, you know. Old Testament characters did it all the time.
Two	Did what?
One	They were honest with God. Yes they praised God, but they also argued with, shouted at, got cross with and generally gave God a hard time – if they felt that was what was necessary. I'm sure God can take it.
Two	I'm sure God can . . . it's just a little bit beyond my experience okay? I was always taught to respect my elders and betters and

they don't get much older or *(Fights for word)* betterer . . . than God.

One   But as soon as you do that you put up barriers between you and the wonderful, loving, close relationship that God wants to have with you. I'd much rather have the odd argument than feel there were things I couldn't say.

Two   I suppose so.

One   Good – you know, I'll have you being honest with God in no time.

Two   Don't count on it.

Stick to it   *Luke 13.31–5*

This first-person monologue is delivered by a witness to Jesus' words in Luke 13. It should be delivered in a conversational style but with deep conviction.

I was there you know . . . that day. Now if you put it alongside all the other days – the extraordinary things that were taking place on a regular basis – it might not seem that what happened on that day was particularly different from any of the others – anything out of the ordinary. It might have seemed that nothing special had taken place. But I do remember it – I remember it quite clearly.

I suppose one of the reasons for that is that it's not every day you hear the king called a 'fox'. I know we were under Roman rule, but still Herod had power, significant power, and people were naturally careful about what they said about him – particularly in mixed, open company – you never knew who might be listening to an unguarded comment. But I don't think there was anything unguarded about the words Jesus used on that particular day. I think his words were very carefully chosen . . . I think he knew exactly what he was doing. It struck me very clearly then – in a way perhaps that it hadn't done before – that nothing . . . I mean nothing . . . was going to stop Jesus doing what he had to do. After all, here were a group of Pharisees telling him that the king was out to kill him and he took it completely in his stride. More than that, he turned it round and made it a criticism of the king himself.

I realized at that point that he was completely determined in a way that very few of us are. Perhaps you're like me. You get a good idea, something that sounds as if it's going to be great, and you throw yourself into it for a while but then as soon as things begin to get just a little bit dull or difficult you give up. Or something else comes along that seems newer – more sparkly – and you follow that instead.

Jesus wasn't like that. He just seemed to know what he wanted to do and did it. Nothing was going to deter him – nothing was going to get in his way, nothing was going to put him off. I wish I had some of that certainty – that dedication to something outside of myself. I sit in absolute awe of it. But Jesus – he knew what was required of him – what was needed – and there wasn't anything that was going to stop that from happening. No matter what.

Third Sunday in Lent Year A

Exodus 17.1–7   Romans 5.1–11   John 4.5–42

Water   *Exodus 17.1–7*
This is a first-person monologue delivered by a slightly tired member of the people of the Israelite nation! No special costuming is necessary.

Well, I can tell you it wasn't before time. I mean I'm not one to complain, really I'm not. Ask any of my friends, they'll tell you. 'Maureen,' they'll say, 'oh she's got a heart of gold that one. She never complains.' And I won't say I haven't had cause over the years. I'm a martyr to my bunions, an absolute martyr. And traipsing through the desert for weeks on end hasn't made them any better. It certainly has not.

My husband, David, he's more inclined to give Moses the benefit of the doubt. 'Give him time,' he says, 'remember how bad things were in Egypt.' I remember how things were in Egypt. He doesn't need to tell me how bad life had become . . . but this? I mean where are we going? Does Moses even know? And what if there are people in this Promised Land, when we get there? What happens then? Do we just go up to them and smile and say, 'Well, I'm terribly sorry, but our God has promised *us* this land, so it's ours now – you'd better leave.' Has anybody thought this through – properly? What they want is a woman in charge. That would soon sort things out.

The latest thing has been the water. How they expect us to travel around in 30-degree heat without any water is beyond me. We're all going to die out here . . . I just know it. So some of the men went to see Moses and told him what was what. 'Get us some water,' they said, 'or we're seriously thinking of striking out on our own.' Well, Moses goes away to pray. I will give him that – he's a very prayerful man – very prayerful indeed. Whether being good at prayer is going to be any help in putting food on the table and water in our mouths, I wouldn't like to say.

Anyway, Moses took some of the leaders with him up the mountain yesterday, carrying a big stick. They came back down an hour later and sent people up the mountainside with buckets to collect the clearest water you ever saw that was just pouring out of some rocks. They said Moses struck the rocks with his stick and the water just appeared.

Well, I don't know about that – appearing/disappearing water – it all sounds very strange to me. My David said we must have faith – he says that God will provide. Well, I don't know about that – if Moses wants me to follow him on this journey, he'll need a bit more than talk of putting faith in God.

Faith and joy   *Romans 5.1–11*

This two-narrator rendering of the words in Romans 5 should be used instead of the reading.

One	We've been put right with God by our faith.
Two	And because of that we live at peace with Jesus.
One	Because of our faith Christ has introduced us to God's undeserved kindness. On which we take our stand.
Two	We are so happy as we look forward to sharing in God's glory!
One	But that's not all!
Two	We rejoice when we run into problems and suffering.
One	Because we know they help us to develop endurance.
Two	And from endurance comes strength of character . . .
One	Which gives us a hope that will never disappoint us.
Two	All of this happens because God loves us and has given us the Holy Spirit . . .
One	To fill our hearts with love.
Two	When we were completely helpless . . .
One	At just the right time . . .
Two	Christ came and died for us.
One	No one is really willing to die for an honest person.
Two	Though someone might be prepared to die for a truly good person.
One	But God showed amazing love for us by sending Christ to die for us . . .
Two	While we were still full of sin.
One	But there is yet more.
Two	Because Christ sacrificed his life's blood for us we have been made safe from God's anger.
One	Even when we were God's enemies, he made peace with us because his Son died for us.

Two	Yet something even greater than friendship is ours.
One	Now that we are at peace with God, we will be saved by his Son's life.
Two	So we can delight in our wonderful new relationship with God, because Jesus has enabled us to be friends with God.

Conversations by wells   *John 4.5–42*

Esther and Rachel are both warm, slightly chatty individuals. They can enter from the audience/congregation in character and then invite the group to listen to their conversation. No special costuming is necessary.

Esther	*(Addressing congregation)* Oh there you are. Come in, come in.
Rachel	You're most welcome . . . really you are.
Esther	Make yourselves comfortable, and we'll tell you all about our friend Sarah.
Rachel	Oh come on now, Esther, let's start by being honest shall we? She wasn't really our friend.
Esther	Well, if we're being truthful, she wasn't anybody's friend.
Rachel	No – the fact of the matter is that our Sarah had got herself a bit of a reputation.
Esther	A BIT of a reputation? She's had five husbands.
Rachel	Five. And she was living with a man who might have become number six.
Esther	Six. Scandalous.
Rachel	Absolutely scandalous.
Esther	That was why she couldn't be our friend you see.
Rachel	Why she had to go and collect her water from the well in the heat of the day, when there wasn't anybody else at the well.
Esther	It wasn't that we didn't like her.
Rachel	We just didn't want to talk to her.
Esther	Well, you can understand, can't you?
Rachel	Of course you can.
Esther	And then there was the day it all changed.
Rachel	I can still remember Sarah running into the town, breathless, excited, shouting to anyone who would listen.
Esther	'Come and meet the man who told me everything I have ever done.'
Rachel	That's what she said – and there was something about how she said it.

Esther	Something about her eyes as well . . .
Rachel	Which made us wonder whether she was telling the truth.
Esther	It turns out she'd had an encounter with a wandering preacher at the well.
Rachel	Name of Jesus.
Esther	When we asked her later what he'd said, one thing in particular stuck in my mind.
Rachel	It's linked with the well.
Esther	He said that he could give her a different kind of water.
Rachel	A source of water that would well up in her life.
Esther	Making sure that she would never be thirsty again.
Rachel	Well, I'm not sure what on earth he was talking about.
Esther	Neither am I, but whatever it was, Sarah is a changed person.
Rachel	Absolutely transformed inside.
Esther	Quite extraordinary.
Rachel	If this is what this new water does . . .
Esther	Then I want some of it for myself.
Rachel	Me too.
Esther	Do you want to join the queue?

Third Sunday in Lent Year B

John 2.13–22 1   Corinthians 1.18–25

The report   *John 2.13–22*

An imaginary TV report from the Temple based on the events in the John reading. The reporter is a fairly typically overly dramatic caricature. Seth is cross about what has happened. No special costuming is necessary.

Reporter	Good morning. You join us here live in the Temple courtyards at the end of what has been a tumultuous morning. In this reporter's long years of experience covering strange events, this has got to be one of the strangest and the most upsetting. Only an hour or so ago a young man who goes by the name of Jesus burst into this most sacred of spaces and caused a riot. I'm joined by Seth Golden, a trader here in the Temple courts who witnessed these stunning events. Seth, in your own words, can you tell me what happened?

Seth	Well, you know, I'd been setting up like any other morning . . .
Reporter	Excuse me, Seth, can I just ask . . . exactly what were you setting up?
Seth	Oh sorry, yeah – ah . . . my money-changing stall.
Reporter	Your money-changing stall? What's wrong with ordinary money?
Seth	Ah well, you see your ordinary shekel isn't holy enough or sacred enough to be used here in the Temple Courts – you have to have Temple money – and that's where I come in see. You give me your everyday money, and I give you some Temple money. At a small handling fee.
Reporter	A 'small' handling fee?
Seth	Well, 25 per cent is small . . . ish.
Reporter	And I suppose that people then put that money into the Temple collection boxes?
Seth	It's not quite as simple as that, sir. No – you then have to go to my friend Harry over there and buy yourself a pigeon to sacrifice at the Temple altar.
Reporter	A pigeon?
Seth	Oh yeah, beautiful they are, bred especially for the purpose – quality merchandise.
Reporter	And you can only buy them with Temple money?
Seth	Absolutely.
Reporter	Excuse me, but what's to stop me from buying my own pigeon outside of the Temple and bringing it in with me?
Seth	Oh no, mate, you can't do that, no, no, no.
Reporter	And why not?
Seth	Well, it's only the pigeons that are sold here in the Temple Courts that are holy enough and sacred enough to be used in Temple services.
Reporter	But they're double the price in here.
Seth	I know . . . holiness doesn't come cheap. And anyway, these Temple concession stands cost a mint. We're giving loads of money to the authorities.
Reporter	I see . . . none of this is very holy, is it?
Seth	What do you mean?
Reporter	Well, the buying and selling, the blatant corruption, the swindling of ordinary people . . . none of that sounds very holy.
Seth	You know, funnily enough, that's what Jesus said.

Reporter	I'm beginning to see his point.
Seth	But he was really angry – he made a whip out of cords and everything.
Reporter	I'm only sorry he beat me to it.
Seth	Does that mean you're not going to pay me for my interview anymore?
Reporter	You've got it in one. Well, there we have it folks. What I thought was a story about violence turns out to be a story about corruption. No doubt we'll be hearing more of this young man called Jesus in the days to come.

Foolish?   1 Corinthians 1.18–25

This meditative set of thoughts on 1 Corinthians 1 is a straight non-dramatic reading and should be treated as such.

It's foolish, isn't it? Stupid. Outrageous. And that's why I love it. We're all so sensible all the time, so po-faced, so logical. We like things that make sense.

We have listened to the world for so long that we think it makes sense. With all of its talk of power and wealth being the only things that matter. We've bought into what the advertisers have been telling us for years . . . that it actually matters what brand of toothpaste you use and what car you drive. We've actually fallen for it – all this talk of stardom and glamour. We have got to the point where we believe that it matters who wins the next reality contestant show.

We have bought the dream, and it's a shoddy one. It's a dream of plastic surgery and 'me' being the only thing that matters, a dream of fake tan and designer labels.

Against all of that God seems so foolish. But it is a delicious foolishness, a wonderful reality. It is a world where love matters, where sacrifice is important. A place where, though thoroughly and completely undeserving, humanity has grace and hope showered down upon it.

To a world obsessed with wealth God says, 'I love the poor.' To a world where power is everything God says, 'I send my son to be powerless and vulnerable.' To a world completely absorbed with its own cleverness God says, 'I love the innocence of children.'

Every idea is turned upside down. Every concept reworked in a new and strange direction. Every notion is spun to face the opposite way. It is foolishness, and it is glorious . . . and it is GOD!

Third Sunday in Lent Year C

Isaiah 55.1–9   Luke 13.1–9

Obsolete?   *Isaiah 55.1–9*

Ralph and Jim are sitting at a table. They are a pair of talking heads who enjoy sharing their general ignorance over a pint.

Ralph	I'm amazed, Jim mate.
Jim	You are, Ralphy boy . . . why's that then?
Ralph	It's my phone, Jim mate.
Jim	Oh yeah? Marvellous piece of technology is it, Ralph?
Ralph	Marvellous is not the word, Jim. 'Marvellous' is doing it an injustice. 'Marvellous' doesn't even go half way to summing up the miracles and wonders that this little device is capable of, mate.
Jim	Oh yeah?
Ralph	Phone, HDTV, video camera, camera, recording device, my entire music collection, diary, alarm, book reader, movie watcher. I think it might even put the kids to bed and make a cup of tea.
Jim	That's good, mate, innit?
Ralph	Good? Good? It's divine, mate . . . but there is a problem.
Jim	What's that then?
Ralph	Well, this model is three minutes old . . .
Jim	Yeah?
Ralph	And it's already obsolete.
Jim	Oh.
Ralph	Yeah – I've just had a text from the manufacturer asking whether I want to upgrade my machine to the latest superior model.
Jim	That's always the way with western consumer society, innit Ralphy boy.
Ralph	Is it?
Jim	Oh absolutely. The whole basis of it is that they've always got to leave you wanting more. They don't want you satisfied mate. Not for one minute.
Ralph	What, you mean I'm never going to be satisfied?

Jim	Well, only for very short periods of time.
Ralph	I'm devastated mate – I'm never going to be happy.
Jim	Ah well, Ralphy boy, if you're going to measure your happiness by the stuff you have – then true enough, you never are going to be happy. You're always going to be unsatisfied.
Ralph	I can feel a 'but' coming here, mate.
Jim	You're right there. Put your trust – put your heart – in other stuff – stuff that lasts, stuff that won't let you down, stuff that won't be obsolete in five minutes' time. Put it in God, mate.
Ralph	You know, Jim – you're right. I'm going to keep this phone so long that it's going to be an embarrassment to my kids. I'm going to spend my time concentrating on stuff that's actually important.
Jim	Well said, Ralph mate, well said.

Second chances   *Luke 13.1–9*

This monologue based on the thoughts and ideas in the Luke reading should be delivered in a conversational style but with real conviction. No special costuming is necessary.

I know he wanted to cut it down right away. He was very clear about that. No confusion. 'Cut it down,' he said, 'cut it down right now.' And who can blame him? I mean it was a pretty sorry specimen. In fact I said so myself to it one morning.

Yes – all right – it's a bit odd, I know – I talk to plants. I think it relieves the tension . . . or perhaps it's because they don't answer back. Anyway, I stared at it one morning, folded my arms, and in the sternest voice that I could muster I said, 'You know, you're really not helping anybody by being such a sorry specimen . . . just grow some fruit will you? GROW!' I think I might have even stamped my foot. Just to show I meant business.

What kind of self-respecting fig tree grows no figs? I mean that's its purpose in life – that's what it's here for – to grow figs. So if you've got a tree that needs to grow figs and that's the one thing it's not doing, how long do you wait? How much space and time and energy do you devote? I know that's what the issue was. But nevertheless I really wanted to give it one more chance. I don't know why. Perhaps I saw something in it that others hadn't – perhaps I'm just a big softie. I don't know. What I do know is that I pleaded for one more chance. I just felt that if we gave it one more year . . . one more growing season . . . then it might come through. It might make good on all the promise. That's what I felt anyway . . . and I went, and I pleaded its case. 'Please,' I said, 'please, just one more year. Just one. Then – if it doesn't produce anything, do what you want with it, cut it down, throw it on the fire. Just give it one last chance.'

So that's what it got. I believe – I firmly believe – in second chances . . . perhaps even third, fourth or fifth chances. And I know that God does too. Do those chances ever run out? And what happens when they do? I don't know. But I will keep on rooting for second chances, for opportunities to surprise and come good, for abundant fruitful life, for the discovery of purpose and meaning. After all . . . who wouldn't want that?

Fourth Sunday in Lent Year A

1 Samuel 16.1–13   John 9.1–41

Samuel remembers   *1 Samuel 16.1–13*
This imagined monologue of the thoughts of Samuel should be delivered briskly and with feeling. No special costuming or props are necessary.

Ah, my dear friends – you have no idea how difficult it was. I had wanted Saul to succeed as King so badly. Who wouldn't? He was just what you would want from a King – wise, thoughtful, brave – at least at the beginning. And, of course, God had been part of the choosing. God used me to anoint him, to choose him above all others. So I was pretty sure the decision was the right one. And so it was . . . until things started to go wrong. It's so difficult to watch someone that you had such high hopes for – such dreams and visions for – slowly unravel before your eyes. It was heartbreaking – a bit like a death in its own way. What I encountered certainly felt a lot like grieving.

So when God told me to get ready because a new king had been chosen, you can imagine how enthusiastic I was . . . not at all! 'I'm sending you to Jesse of Bethlehem,' God said. 'Choose someone else,' I said! 'If Saul hears of this, I'm as good as dead,' I said. But I'm afraid God doesn't take 'no' for an answer. So off I went to meet Jesse and his sons. And I have to admit then when I saw his eldest, Eliab, I thought, 'This is it.' He was ideal: tall, dignified, handsome – just what you might want in a king. But, of course, he wasn't the one God had picked. Why did I think it was going to be that easy? 'Pay no attention to outward appearance,' I heard that familiar voice say. Seven sons later I was still waiting for God to say 'yes'. I was getting tired and fractious by this stage, I don't mind telling you. Was God ever going to choose one? Each one was younger and smaller and less likely than the last.

I looked at Jesse in despair, 'Have you got any more sons?' I pleaded. Well, it turns out there was one just one more. In came the last boy – name of David. Oh, he was handsome, with ruddy cheeks and bright eyes but oh so young. 'He's the one,' said the voice. So he's the one – the anointed King. I don't mind telling you he wasn't my choice. I was looking for someone more like Saul. More like the picture of a king I have in my mind. Someone who is closer to what we have had in the past. But that's God for you. Always upsetting expectations, always choosing the last person you'd expect.

The closer I get – the more surprising God becomes. It's exasperating, thrilling, exciting and scary all at the same time. It's just as well I stick close – because you never know where we're going next.

Seeing and not seeing *John 9.1–41*

A Pharisee is sitting on one side of a table, the man born blind is seated opposite. The Pharisee is trying to be personable but cannot stop being slightly threatening. The Blind Man is confused but delighted. No special costuming is needed, but you will need two chairs and a table.

Pharisee	All I want, and I'm sure you'll understand this, is a little reassurance. That's not too much to ask for in these troubled times, is it? A little reassurance?
Blind man	I'm not sure I know what you mean.
Pharisee	All right, it's like this. We have people telling us that you were born blind. Now that can't be right, can it? Because clearly you can see.
Blind man	I've told you time and time again. The story isn't going to change. Yes, I was born blind. I'm well known in and around the city – ask anybody.
Pharisee	Well, that's part of my problem you see – we've got some conflicting reports on that. Maybe you can help me. We've got some people who claim that you are the blind person they've seen begging on various street corners around the city, and there are others who say that you're not that person at all – you just look like him. Now, which am I to believe?
Blind man	Well, it's clear to me what's happening. I'm surprised a man of your intelligence hasn't spotted it.
Pharisee	Oh yes? And what has a beggar spotted that I haven't?
Blind man	They can't believe their own eyes. They don't want to admit – to see what has actually happened – because that would mean they'd

have to change the way they look at the world – the way they understand it.

Pharisee	Well, you can hardly blame their uncertainty, can you? I mean, people born blind normally stay that way.
Blind man	It also means that they'd have to think carefully about the person who gave me my sight.
Pharisee	Ah yes, now you see: that's another thing I'm interested in ... Jesus. You say he was the one who gave you your sight.
Blind man	I do.
Pharisee	And you're sure you don't want to rethink that answer? Things could get very complicated for you if you don't.
Blind man	I know how much you hate him – how angry he's made you. But that's not going to change what happened. *(Quietly)* Jesus gave me my sight.
Pharisee	I can see a certain degree of stubbornness beginning to show itself. I will talk with you later when you've had time to reconsider your options.
Blind man	I was blind – I haven't seen anything in my entire life – but I could see Jesus – I could see the kind of person he was – the power and grace and love. You've been able to see your entire life yet you can't see what's right in front of your nose.
Pharisee	Yes ... well, let's just leave the homespun wisdom at home, shall we. Let's see what a few hours in a nice dark cell will do for you. After all, if you're telling the truth and you were born blind – you'll feel right at home. If I were you, I'd think through my options very carefully – very carefully indeed.

Fourth Sunday in Lent Year B

Ephesians 2.1–10   John 3.14–21

Free   *Ephesians 2.1–10*
A shopkeeper stands centrally behind a counter (table) – a customer enters. The shopkeeper and customer are bright and friendly. No special costuming is necessary, but a paper bag is needed.

Shopkeeper	Ah, good morning, good morning, what can I do for you?
Customer	I'll have a nice big helping of grace please.

Shopkeeper	Certainly . . . and if I might say so . . . what a very good choice you've made. *(Produces paper bag)* There you are, just as ordered . . . a nice big helping of grace. Should keep you going ages, that should.
Customer	So how much do I owe you?
Shopkeeper	Excuse me?
Customer	How much coinage of the realm should I be handing over for this fine purchase?
Shopkeeper	Oh, sorry sir/madam, I thought you understood. Grace is free.
Customer	I'm sorry – I don't think I heard you properly.
Shopkeeper	It's free . . . gratis . . . no charge expected or made.
Customer	Well, that can't be right.
Shopkeeper	What can't be right?
Customer	Well, this . . . it can't be free.
Shopkeeper	Can't it?
Customer	Well, no . . . because then anybody could have it.
Shopkeeper	You've got it in one . . . anybody CAN have it.
Customer	Well, then it can't be very valuable.
Shopkeeper	On the contrary sir/madam, it is about the most valuable thing you could ever hope to possess.
Customer	Well, then it must cost something.
Shopkeeper	Not to you it doesn't.
Customer	Well, have you got a premium edition of grace . . . something that I can buy that will mark me out from the crowd?
Shopkeeper	No, I'm sorry, it's one size fits all.
Customer	But there must be something I can do?
Shopkeeper	I don't catch your drift.
Customer	I must be able to do something to pay for it, be worthy of it. Perhaps I could earn it in some way . . . perhaps you've got some dishes at the back that need washing up?
Shopkeeper	*(Getting increasingly frustrated)* Look sir/madam, you're very nice but we're going to fall out about this in a minute. This is grace – it is the most valuable thing you could ever hope to possess and it is absolutely free of charge. That is . . . free. You cannot earn it, be worthy of it, or pay for it in any way. At the very real possibility of being a tad boring . . . am I making myself crystal clear?
Customer	*(Pause)* Perhaps if there was a payment plan?
Shopkeeper	Argghh! *(Customer exits leaving paper bag behind)*

Love   *John 3.14–21*

Jenny is writing a letter and reads aloud. No special costuming is necessary. The style is conversational and bright.

Dear Julie,

It's not going to be easy writing this, because I think I'm lining myself up for the biggest 'I told you so' moment of all time. Do you remember – it was about five years ago I think – when you told me that Christianity is really quite simple?

I didn't believe you at the time. I'd got to a point where I wanted everything to be deep and full of purpose. I'd got it into my head that religion had to involve something really dramatic or it couldn't be worth anything. Everywhere I looked I saw drama and crisis, and I thought any religion worth its salt must be about that too. 'I can't take Christianity seriously,' I thought to myself. 'It doesn't ask me to go through anything like enough angst.' When I think back to how I was then . . . I don't know how anybody put up with me for more than five minutes at a time.

'No,' you said. 'Christianity's simpler than that – it's all about love.' Of course, I didn't believe you at the time. How could anything be about an idea so simple, so naive? There must be more to it than that. So I gave up – as you well know . . . I had a talent for giving things up in those days.

It's taken some time of looking in other places and not finding anything for me to come back full circle to where I started. Now I don't think I've got all the answers yet (in fact I'm certain I haven't). There are still massive holes in my understanding – but I have managed to grasp this one idea. Granted it's the biggest idea ever . . . it's the idea that everything else hangs on. And as you said (here comes the 'I told you so' moment), it really is all about love. I can't believe I was so blind to it before.

We are loved – amazingly, completely, shockingly, awe-inspiringly loved. Loved beyond anything we can understand. Loved with a passion and intensity that is incredible. Loved by the one who made the universe and everything in it – and all we have to do is show love in return – love to God and love to each other. Granted we're not very good at our part of that equation. We make excuses not to love. We count people out, we see them as different. We find a million different little reasons every day why we can't love particular people. But even our failure to do that doesn't stop God loving us. It really is extraordinary.

So, thank you, Julie. Thank you for telling me the truth all those years ago, and I'm sorry it's taken me so long to come round finally. Thank you for keeping me in your prayers (because I know you've been doing that). I guess God (and you!) are more patient than me.

I'll see you soon.

Love,

Jenny

Fourth Sunday in Lent Year C

2 Corinthians 5.16–21   Luke 15.1–3, 11b–32

Ambassador Claire   *2 Corinthians 5.16–21*

This dramatic monologue should be delivered with conviction. Claire is one of those older saintly people in many churches who are lacking in confidence in their own value.

I have to tell you I don't feel very much like an ambassador. Not very much like an ambassador at all. I've been going to church for about five or six years now – ever since my husband died. They were ever so kind and welcoming. They went out of their way . . . sent me a card after the funeral. The minister even came two or three weeks afterwards to see how I was doing.

Well, I thought to myself . . . why not? I've always been interested in religion . . . in God . . . and they've been so lovely. Why not try it out? And I haven't looked back since. I've got really involved. I go to the Women's Meeting and the Coffee Morning, and I've even put myself down on the church cleaning rota. And then, of course, there's the Sunday services. They're lovely, and I've learned ever such a lot from listening to the sermons. And singing the hymns . . . well, I can't tell you how much that's meant to me. I've met such a lot of lovely people. And it's been really important for me. My Jack and I – we spent so much time with each other that I hadn't really made that many friends outside of our home and family. Well, the church has seen to that. I've got lots of new friends, and if I'm not there for any reason, there's always somebody who will check to make sure that I'm all right.

That's all well and good. But sometimes I feel I ought to be doing more. There was a service in church the other Sunday, when the preacher told us we were all ambassadors for Jesus. Well, I thought, I don't know about that. I'm not really sure I feel like an ambassador. It sounds very grand. Ambassadors represent somebody, don't they? Well, I'm not sure that I'm a very good representative of Jesus. I try . . . I really do . . . but there's so much I still don't understand . . . so much I'm not sure of. And I'm really not a very confident person. Being an ambassador frightens me.

Well, I got myself all upset about it and then I saw my friend Joan, and I told her how worried I was. 'Oh, Claire, you daft thing,' she said, 'you're already an ambassador.' Well, I didn't know what she meant, but then she went on to remind me that a year or so ago I'd invited my next-door neighbour Christine to church. She was a bit lonely, and I told her how much of a change it had made to me, and I said to her, 'Look, if you're not sure, why don't you come to the Coffee Morning first? I'll come round, and we can go together.' She did just that, and she's been coming ever since. She comes on a Sunday as well, and she's really enjoying it – she's ever so keen to find out more.

It turns out I'm an ambassador after all. All it needs is for you to recognize other people who need God's love and invite them in as well. When you put it like that . . . well, not so daunting after all. In fact, I'm quite enjoying it . . . me, an ambassador . . . fancy that?

Brothers *Luke 15.1–3, 11b–32*
The two brothers from the parable are seated facing the audience – they do not acknowledge each other but speak directly to the audience as if responding to interview questions. No special costuming is necessary.

Younger I have to say that I'd got to the end of my tether. The depth of my stupidity and selfishness had really begun to dawn on me. I was sitting there surrounded by pigs . . . pigs for goodness' sake. What on earth had I been thinking? To have thrown so much away, to have sunk so low. It was then that I made up my mind to go home.

Older I don't like to speak ill of him, but it was actually quite nice without him. He'd always been different . . . never quite fitted in. Always flighty, thinking of himself, never interested in the work needed to keep the farm successful. Without him . . . life was simpler. There were fewer arguments. Not that Dad ever argued with him . . . but I did . . . all the time.

Younger If I think about it now, even going home was an act of calculation – a selfish move. There I was on the road home rehearsing what I was going to say, trying to get the words just right. I have to accept that I was returning because I'd run out of places to go – I was desperate. It isn't very noble, is it?

Older If you were to ask me if I'm proud of what I've achieved here, I'd say 'yes', absolutely. I've worked hard . . . done what was asked of me. If you were to ask me whether I approve of what he did . . . taking everything and leaving, then I'd have to say 'no'. I've never understood him, and I don't think I ever will. And it's been hard for me seeing clearly how much Dad obviously misses him – how he pines for him.

Younger So there I was – walking up the path – speech rehearsed and ready – when Dad races down the path to meet me, flings his

	arms around my neck and gives me a huge hug. He threw his own dignity out the door to save my embarrassment. I think it was then that I began to realize that what I had missed most, what I had needed most was not the food, not the comfort of being at home, but his love.
Older	What am I meant to say? How am I meant to act? It's clear that my father's love is bigger and more forgiving than mine could ever be. And I can't help feeling that there is a lesson here that I am only slowly beginning to learn. My father's love reaches out and embraces people who are incredibly different from me – people who quite honestly I don't like. And that is . . . something that I am going to have to learn from . . . and embrace.

The brothers look at each other and exit together.

Fifth Sunday in Lent Year A

Ezekiel 37.1–14   John 11.1–45

Dry bones   *Ezekiel 37.1–14*

A TV morning chat-show presenter is seated and addresses the congregation. Ezekiel is straightforward and honest. No special costuming is necessary. Two chairs are needed.

Presenter	Now if I asked you – 'Have you ever had a vision?' I guess most of you would say, 'Only when I've had a bit too much wine to drink on a Saturday night', but my guest this morning has recently claimed to have had the most amazing vision, and it involves the most extraordinary thing . . . bones. Please welcome feisty prophet Ezekiel.

Applause, Ezekiel enters and sits

Ezekiel	Good morning.
Presenter	Good morning – well, Ezekiel, this all sounds rather strange. Are you in the habit of seeing visions of bones on a regular basis?
Ezekiel	No . . . of course not.
Presenter	So tell me what happened on this particular occasion?
Ezekiel	Well, the Lord came to me . . .
Presenter	The Lord? Are you in the habit of having visions from God?
Ezekiel	Well, I am a prophet.

Presenter	Indeed – just giving the folks at home the opportunity to make some snap judgements about you in their minds . . . carry on.
Ezekiel	As I was saying – the Lord came to me and took me to a very dry plain that was absolutely full of bones. And the Lord said to me, 'Can these bones live again?'
Presenter	Well, that's a bit weird, isn't it? What a question to ask!
Ezekiel	That's what I thought – which was why I answered, 'Only you know that.'
Presenter	But I think it's what happened next that's really going to surprise our viewers . . .
Ezekiel	Well, God told me to prophesy to the bones – so I did. And they started twitching and coming together, and sinew and flesh and skin began to appear.
Presenter	This is all beginning to sound a bit macabre.
Ezekiel	And then God told me to prophesy again, and wind came – breathing life into the bodies.
Presenter	This is all very strange, if you don't mind my saying so.
Ezekiel	I've thought about it a lot since.
Presenter	I'm sure you have.
Ezekiel	And I keep coming back to the same question.
Presenter	Oh yes . . . and what's that?
Ezekiel	What is life?
Presenter	I beg your pardon?
Ezekiel	Do we sleepwalk through life, feeling dry and lifeless? Never really doing what God requires of us . . . never really doing anything of worth at all? Or are we going to open ourselves up so that God can breathe life into us and give us the purpose and direction we need?
Presenter	Goodness. Well, there you have it ladies and gentlemen – a tortured prophet, a valley of bones and the most extraordinary vision . . . what do you make of it? Holy revelation or the ranting of a mad man? You decide – you can email, text or phone us, contact us on Twitter on find us on Facebook.

Life   *John 11.1–45*

This imaginary dramatic monologue is delivered by the caterer at Lazarus' funeral. A sentence of introduction for the audience/congregation might be helpful. No special costuming is necessary.

Nobody ever thinks about the poor little self-employed businessman do they? Trying to scratch out a living in today's economic climate – well, it's bad enough without what happened last week. I mean it's disastrous, that's what it is. Worst of all, it makes me look like a fool, calls into doubt my professionalism, and I'll have you know you won't find a better funeral director this side of Jerusalem.

My family have been in the business for years, my father and his father before him. We've built up a well-deserved reputation for our dignity and our caring service. Our funeral teas are the best in town – our fishpaste sandwiches are little pieces of heaven on a plate. And now? Now it's all round the town that I can't even tell when a body is dead or not. I tell you – this is not fair – not fair at all. I personally met with the family on several occasions before the funeral. I put into place all the arrangements. I saw Lazarus on three separate occasions, before we put his body in the tomb, and I tell you now – without a shadow of a doubt – Lazarus was dead. His sisters Martha and Mary – they'll tell you. They'll vouch for my professional opinion – he was dead.

It's just so annoying . . . oh now don't get me wrong. I'm sure they're happy enough – Martha and Mary I mean – in fact I know they are. They've invited me round to their house for tea next week. I'm almost hoping that Lazarus won't be there. It could all get rather awkward. I mean, how do you make polite conversation with a man you buried? You tell me that. It's all in slightly poor taste.

It's that Jesus I blame. Coming along and meddling when he wasn't wanted. 'Lazarus,' he says, 'come out.' And I'm thinking, 'Well, that's hardly likely. I attended to the funeral wrappings with my own fair hands.' But then there he was – standing at the entrance of his own tomb – bold as you like. My heart sank.

I have to say that Lazarus has a remarkably healthy appetite for a man in his situation – he tucked into the cheesy puffs with great gusto. It was just as well we had some left over from the funeral meal.

As for Jesus – he said he'd done it so that people would believe. Well, I don't know what I believe. But the faster he moves on to another community – the faster I can work on rebuilding my business. Fishpaste sandwich anybody?

Fifth Sunday in Lent Year B

Jeremiah 31.31–4   John 12.20–33

Jeremiah reflects   *Jeremiah 31.31–4*
This dramatic monologue is some imagined thoughts of Jeremiah. He is warm and conversational. No special costuming is necessary.

Ah, now then, it is good to see you . . . gather round: I have a question to ask of you. Do you know what it's like to have your words misinterpreted? Do you? You say something or you write something down and suddenly you realize that people have completely misunderstood what you were trying to say. I can see from your faces that you know . . . that you understand what it is like to have that happen. Frustrating, isn't it? You know what the words were meant to say – what they were trying to convey – but somehow, somewhere along the way they got taken out of context or deliberately twisted.

That happened to me. I wrote some words about God making a new covenant – a new agreement with his people. I wrote about God writing his words on people's hearts. And people took them as being words of ease – words of comfort. They thought, 'Oh well, that's good . . . I don't have to do anything . . . if God is going to write words on my heart then it's all up to God – I can just sit back and let it happen.'

How foolish some people are! I only wrote that because the people had been so wilful, so disobedient. It wasn't meant to make them feel comfortable or happy with their lot. What I was trying to say was that they had broken the covenant so many times that the only way forward was for God to tear it up . . . make an absolutely new beginning, a fresh start – write something in such a way that they couldn't destroy it or make a mess of it.

Now you see, I know what you're going to ask next. I can see it on your faces. Yes, I can. You're going to say to me, 'That's all very well, Jeremiah. All of this talk of new starts and fresh beginnings – it sounds wonderful. But what is this new start? How will we recognize it? What is God going to do?' And I would answer you . . . I don't know. I'm sorry, I know it's frustrating. I know God is planning some way of saving us from our own ignorance, our own wilful disobedience, our own inability to do the right thing – the good thing – the just thing. I know God is planning to provide us with hope, with a completely new start. I know that God is planning to give us a whole new way to have a relationship with the creative force behind all things. But how is God going to do that? I don't know. I wish I did.

Still – that should give us hope, shouldn't it? God providing us with a way to get ourselves out of the mess we have got ourselves into? It all sounds pretty hopeful to me.

I want to see Jesus   *John 12.20–33*
Sarah is a regular church attendee not used to talking about what her faith means to her. Alisha is a new visitor – friendly but direct. Sarah is standing centrally, Alisha enters.

Alisha	Hi, do you go to this church?
Sarah	Um . . . er, well, yes I do actually . . . when I can . . . you know.
Alisha	Good – I want to see Jesus, and I was wondering whether you could help me.
Sarah	I beg your pardon?
Alisha	I've been getting more and more interested in finding out about Christianity recently, and I was wondering whether you could tell me about your faith, talk to me about why Jesus is so important to you – show me Jesus.
Sarah	Oh, um . . . yes . . . well. I think you'd better talk to our minister about that – she'll be here in half an hour or so. She's ever so nice – I'm sure she'll be able to help you.
Alisha	No offence – but I'd rather not talk to a minister or a pastor or a vicar – I was hoping that I could talk to an ordinary member of the congregation about what Jesus means to them in their every-day lives.
Sarah	Oh dear – do you . . . really? Wouldn't you rather go to our Women's Fellowship Group? I gather they've got ever such an interesting talk on tea towels this afternoon.
Alisha	If it's all the same to you, I'd rather hear about Jesus.
Sarah	What about our coffee morning? There's always loads of people you can sit and have a chat with there – it's every Friday morning. They serve Fairtrade goods, you know.
Alisha	But Friday's in three days' time. I want someone to show me Jesus now.
Sarah	Oh dear.
Alisha	I'm beginning to think you don't want to show me Jesus at all. Does he not mean very much to you?
Sarah	It's not that . . . honestly. It's just that you're the first person who's ever asked me that question. I've never really talked about my faith before. I'm not sure I'll say the right thing.
Alisha	I'm sure you'll be fine . . . just speak honestly . . . from the heart.
Sarah	Um . . . yes . . . easier said than done I'm afraid. Are you sure you wouldn't like to wait for the minister? She really is lovely.
Alisha	I'm sure she is. But I'd rather hear it from you.
Sarah	Goodness . . . God-talk . . . Jesus . . . what does Jesus mean to me . . . ?
Alisha	Look, you'll be fine. But if I'm going to take Christianity seriously . . . if I'm going to come to this church, I want to have a sense that

it will be worth it. I want to know that the faith, the spirituality of people here is real . . . alive. I want to know that Jesus actually makes a difference to the way you live your life . . . show me Jesus in you.

Sarah   Okay – come on inside then . . . I'll put the kettle on. What Jesus means to me . . . where on earth to start . . . there's so much. *They exit.*

Fifth Sunday in Lent Year C

Philippians 3.4b–14   John 12.1–8

Choice   *Philippians 3.4b–14*
Two actors stand centrally and speak with each other. This simple two-narrator dialogue emphasizes the issues of choice raised by the Philippians passage. It should be delivered briskly and with energy. No special costuming is necessary.

One	You could choose something else you know.
Two	No, I couldn't.
One	Of course you could – just think of all the other options you have open to you.
Two	Oh yes, like what?
One	Well, I don't know, you could choose fame you know – that's always a really popular choice. Think *X Factor* with actual talent. You could be the next singing sensation or paparazzi target. Think of it – coming out of select nightclubs at 3 a.m., flashes going off everywhere . . . how exciting.
Two	Uh, I don't think so.
One	Or what about money? That's always brilliant. You don't even have to have the fame to go with it – just the ability to buy anything you want. 'I think I'll just buy that Bentley over there.' That's got to be an attractive option.
Two	Again, no thank you.
One	Okay – you've got to want power. Who doesn't want power? You could order people around all day, influence the lives of thousands if not millions of people. How fantastic would that be?
Two	No. Honestly . . . no.
One	So you're going to stick with your original choice?
Two	Yes.

One	There's really nothing I can do that will encourage you to change your mind?
Two	Absolutely nothing.
One	This is all very odd. You're going to choose Jesus?
Two	Every time.
One	Even when life is really difficult?
Two	Especially then.
One	Even when flashing some cash around could get you out of a really tricky spot?
Two	Look . . . what is it that you don't understand? I choose Jesus. Every day when I get up, I choose Jesus. When life is terrible and I feel completely alone, I choose Jesus. When things seem like an uphill struggle, and I don't think I'm ever going to get to the finishing line in one piece, I choose Jesus. In every possible situation in any conceivable circumstance, I choose Jesus.
One	All right, I get the idea.
Two	Good – I wouldn't want there to be any misunderstanding.
One	*(Pause)* Now, you're sure?
Two	Argghh! For me there is no other possible choice.
One	Okay . . . okay . . . just asking.

Mary remembers   *John 12.1–8*

This simple dramatic monologue imagines the thoughts of Mary. It should be delivered with commitment and restrained feeling. No special costuming is necessary.

I don't think it comes to all of us and in that sense I guess I hold myself really fortunate that it did happen to me. But for some of us I think there comes a time when you really just recognize what is actually important in your life and what isn't.

Sometimes it happens over a long period of time – events happen and you gradually begin to see clearly and properly what matters. I think for other people it happens suddenly in a kind of flash of inspiration. For some people, it's a brush with illness or death that means you suddenly see things with crystal clarity; for others, it's chance encounters or some other life-changing event.

It's strange – I'd known Jesus for some time. He'd changed my world, the way I understand everything. I'd seen him do things that would take your breath away. But as the days and weeks went by I began to be aware of something else. I don't know what to call it – an ending? A climax? All the strands of what was happening seemed to be coming together very quickly . . . building to something that made me very frightened indeed. If I had thought that trying to talk Jesus out of whatever was coming would have helped, I would have done that. But I'd been around Jesus long enough to know that once he'd set his mind on something, that was it. And anyway, I had this feeling that what he was about to do was as important for me – for everybody – as it was for him. Perhaps I just ought to let him do it.

Suddenly for me there was nothing more important than showing Jesus that I understood, that in some small way I'd got it. He'd get so frustrated with us when we didn't understand. I suddenly realized that at that moment – in that tiny pinprick of space and time – the only thing that mattered was showing that I understood and that I loved and worshipped him.

And so I got the perfume, and for those few precious moments nothing else mattered, not the thought of the cost, nor the sneering of Judas, nor the shocked expressions on the faces of the others. All that mattered was recognizing what I had in front of me and realizing that this and ONLY this was important.

It is vital, I have discovered, every day to recognize what is important in life – really important – and to do something about it. Because if we don't . . . what is life about?

Sixth Sunday in Lent (Palm Sunday) Year A

Philippians 2.5–11   Matthew 21.1–11

Clifton Moore in *Servant of the World*   *Philippians 2.5–11*
Clifton Moore, Hollywood superstar, is talking to his agent, A. J. Don't worry about fighting with an American accent. The air of pomposity and self-entitlement is more important than the nationality.

A. J.	Okay, Mr Moore, I've got a really exciting offer that's just come in from Paramount.
Clifton	Ah, Paramount Studios – I have done some of my finest work for them, you know. Who can forget my towering performance in *Get me to the Church Part 3*?
A. J.	Indeed, Mr Moore. Who would have thought they'd work out a third way for your character to be late for his own wedding?
Clifton	It was all in the performance, A. J. I had to feel the truth of the predicament.
A. J.	Yes . . . anyway, this new role promises to be a great one for you, Mr Moore. They want you to play . . . Jesus.
Clifton	*(Instantly interested)* They do?

A. J.	Yes indeed. They're thinking that it's time we had another biblical epic, and they want to call this one, *Servant of the World*.
Clifton	And because they wanted someone of great spirituality and ethereal holiness, they thought of me?
A. J.	Well, kind of, Mr Moore, but I'm afraid you may have to audition for this role.
Clifton	Audition? Why that's preposterous – I haven't auditioned for a lead since 1996.
A. J.	What can I say, Mr Moore . . . there are some executives at the studio who don't think you're the right person for the role. They're wanting to emphasize the fact that Jesus saw his ministry as one of being a humble servant, and they don't think you can play that.
Clifton	What? Not play a servant? How difficult can it be? Why I've got seven or eight servants of my own – I'll just study them . . . what's the name of that Mexican who cleans my swimming pool?
A. J.	Felipe, Mr Moore . . . and that's just the problem . . . there are one or two at the Studio who don't think you can be humble enough.
Clifton	Humble enough? Humble enough?! Wasn't I humble when I picked up my BAFTA award for long-running recurring role in a daytime soap opera?
A. J.	Well, actually, Mr Moore, you spoke for 15 minutes and didn't thank anybody else.
Clifton	That's because all the others were talentless ingrates.
A. J.	Look, Mr Moore – all I can say is that the scriptwriters have been reading the Bible . . .
Clifton	*(Interrupting)* Why on earth would they want to do that?
A. J.	*(Ignoring him)* And they've discovered that humility and the nature of a servant is central to all that Jesus was in his words and actions.
Clifton	Good grief. Well, A. J., I'll just have to convince them that I am the greatest actor of my generation, the person born to play this role. They couldn't possibly think of anybody else.
A. J.	Humble . . . Mr Moore, keep it humble.
Clifton	Oh, yes, of course. But there are my requirements to be considered . . . the biggest trailer on set, my name above the title of the movie on all publicity, and my fee . . . we mustn't forget my fee . . .
A. J.	*(Long suffering as always)* Yes, Mr Moore.

What would you do? *Matthew 21.1–11*

This dramatic monologue imagines the thoughts of someone from the crowd in the events described by Matthew and the ease of getting swept up by emotion. It should be delivered with conviction and an underlying sense of anger.

I know what you're going to say. Really I do. It's not that difficult to work it out. Of course, it's okay for you. You've got the benefit of distance and hindsight. You can sit there and say, 'Well, I wouldn't have done that. I'd have behaved differently.' Oh really? Would you indeed? I'd love to put you in my place and put that little theory to the test. My guess is you'd do exactly the same as I did – and so many others. Now don't get me wrong – I'm not proud of what happened. It was stupid, cowardly. I thought I was better than that. But when everybody else is doing the same thing . . . when the atmosphere is so charged – well, I challenge anyone not to get swept up by it. On both occasions just for a second I really believed what I was shouting for as well.

Take the Sunday – what a day. Passover approaching, the crowds building up, there was always tension in the air, but this year . . . you could cut it with a knife. The Romans were nervous – soldiers everywhere fingering their swords as though they were ready to draw them at a seconds notice. And then Jesus arrives – and on a donkey as well. Anybody who knew about Jesus and knew their scripture wouldn't take long putting two and two together and coming up with 20. This was it. The moment we'd been waiting for. The news spread like wildfire. Everybody seemed to know what was happening almost immediately. A crowd appeared out of nowhere. Branches were stripped off trees and waved, cheering started. 'Hosanna,' they shouted, 'God bless him who comes in the name of the Lord.' Oh it was a real party atmosphere. We felt things were really about to change. We were up for it – let's take on the world! At that moment I believed that Jesus was the one – that we would do whatever he wanted us to. It was the most exhilarating feeling. Extraordinary.

But then the rest of the week happened. Well, it didn't really. Nothing changed. There was no revolution. No overturning of the government. Jesus came into the city every day and went to the temple, and taught and answered questions. But no action – no attempt to capitalize on what had happened on Sunday. He had the crowd in his hand and he let that go. I have to tell you, by the Friday we were feeling more than let down. We were really angry. All those hopes and dreams dashed. All those beliefs shattered. I tell you – when Pilate brought Jesus out onto the balcony on Friday and offered to free him as an act of mercy for the Passover – we knew what to do. Almost as one voice we shouted back, 'Give us Barabbas!' Am I proud of what happened? Certainly not. Would you have behaved differently if you'd been there? I know you like to think that you would. Keep believing that if you want – but the truth of it is . . . you'd have done exactly the same.

Sixth Sunday in Lent (Palm Sunday) Year B

Philippians 2.5–11   Mark 11.1–11

Mystery   *Philippians 2.5–11*
This simple poetic meditative reading should be delivered at a gentle pace as if telling a story.

He sat at her feet and listened intently as she told her tale.
He listened because she told the tale well.
She paused just long enough at all the right places.
She knew the story well and used words beautifully – occasionally throwing in slightly unusual ones to keep his interest.
But it was more than her telling a good story well that gripped his imagination.
It wasn't that she fully believed every word she said – that much was obvious.
It wasn't even that she convinced him by her words that all she said was true.
It was that the story resonated with something deep inside him.
There was something in him that responded to it.
He knew as soon as she had started that these events needed to happen.
They were part of the story of how the world was and how it needed to be.
How did he know that?
How did he know that this story of immense love and shocking sacrifice was written into the fabric of creation?
How did he know that these events had happened for him?
He was confused but certain at the same time.
What he knew beyond ordinary knowledge was that God had acted.
God – that being that had created the universe had taken action to save him.
That action had come at tremendous and frightening cost.
He also knew that in order to do that God had inhabited a human body.
He did not pretend knowledge that he did not have.
He did not know how it had been achieved . . . or presume to be able to explain it.
He just knew – in some place deep inside himself –
That the story was for him . . .
And the story was true.

A very strange day   *Mark 11.1–11*

Two Roman soldiers are speaking to each other. They are warm and chatty. No special costuming is necessary. Severus is on stage first – Marcus can enter from the main body of the audience/congregation.

Marcus	Greetings, Severus, how are you this fine day, mate?
Severus	Never better, Marcus, coming off guard duty in Jerusalem has got to be the best feeling in the world.
Marcus	Oh don't tell me, mate, I know. These people are potty – I can't fathom them at all. Did you see what happened at the gates today?
Severus	What . . . not that commotion with the palm leaves and the crowd?
Marcus	You got it in one, mate. I mean . . . am I going mad? What on earth was all that about?
Severus	Ah well – I wasn't sure. So I asked one of them. I pulled him to one side and said, 'Okay then, what's all the fuss about, mate?' Do you know what he said?
Marcus	Go on . . . nothing surprises me anymore.
Severus	Well, this guy turns to me – serious as you like – and he says, 'We're cheering that guy on the donkey over there.' I said, 'Oh yeah . . . why's that then?' And he says, 'BECAUSE he's riding a donkey.'
Marcus	They were cheering a guy for riding a donkey?
Severus	Yeah – I mean hold the presses – hot news just in . . . 'Man rides Donkey'!
Marcus	There's got to be more to it than that, hasn't there?
Severus	Well, I pressed him a bit and he said it was the fulfilment of one of their prophecies.
Marcus	They've got a prophecy about a guy riding a donkey? Are you serious? I've got a prophecy for them – man eats chicken! Woman walks across road! Why haven't they got decent prophecies like volcanoes erupting? Earthquakes causing the end of civilization as we know it? Now those are proper prophecies. Something you can really get your teeth into.
Severus	As long as I live I swear I will never understand these people. As if there aren't hundreds of people riding donkeys into Jerusalem every week. What's so special about this one?
Marcus	Ah well, now that I can tell you.

Severus	Oh okay, carry on . . . enlighten me.
Marcus	Well, it's Jesus, innit?
Severus	It's who?
Marcus	Jesus – the preacher from up in Galilee. He's been making his way down to Jerusalem for weeks now. Word is he's going to overthrow us Romans.
Severus	I'd like to see him try. Actually that'd be great . . . if we were kicked out I could go home and I wouldn't have to look at your ugly mug every day.
Marcus	Thanks very much. But this Jesus had better watch it. Word is that the knives are out, and their chief priests are just looking for an opportunity to bring him in.
Severus	Well, after the commotion he caused today they won't be looking for long.
Marcus	Just what we need . . . more work. Come on Severus – back to it. *(Exits)*
Severus	Oooh, you're such a taskmaster. Coming.

Sixth Sunday in Lent (Palm Sunday) Year C

Isaiah 50.4–9a   Luke 19.28–40

Listening   *Isaiah 50.4–9a*
This simple meditative piece can be divided between two or more speakers and should be delivered as a straight reading.

Quiet.
Just for a moment.
Only for a short time.
Silence . . .
Just enough time and space to listen.
Our world is so noisy – chatter and sound everywhere.
Oppressive – deafening – difficult to escape.
Oh for a moment to stop, be still and listen.
Listen to the sounds that flow all around us.
Hear quiet words of wisdom spoken softly.
Catch the voice of the spirit as it prompts us forward.
Wonder at the word of God as at last you hear it.

Listen carefully for the word and put it into action.

For only if you listen to God will you ever know what is needed.

How can you follow if you do not listen first?

It is in faithful listening that everything else falls into place.

So in the silence, listen.

Let God draw close.

And something happens in the opening up.

A transformation takes place in the quietness.

And suddenly in our lives it as if we step to one side and make room.

Make room for God to be seen and heard.

In the words that we say, in the actions that we take . . .

It is as if God is the one who is felt and seen and heard.

And because of that listening, because of that silence

We are able to teach God to all who will hear.

Has it finally come? *Luke 19.28–40*

Sarah and Mark enter talking excitedly. They are disciples who have witnessed the events of the day and finally believe the time of Jesus is coming. No special costuming is necessary.

Sarah	It was when the people at the side of the road started joining in – that's when it really took off.
Mark	Ah, it was fantastic, wasn't it? All the cheering and the shouting – I never want this day to end. 'Hosanna! God bless him who comes in God's name.'
Sarah	Did you see that little girl who climbed up into the tree? I was so scared she was going to fall down or something.
Mark	And that group of old men on the corner as we turned towards the city – shouting so loudly – they'll be completely hoarse tomorrow.
Sarah	Oh . . . it was everything I've dreamed of.
Mark	And at the beginning of Passover as well. The Romans certainly won't be able to ignore this.
Sarah	We should start thinking about how we're going to make the most of this – really take this advantage to open the eyes of the people.
Mark	Did you see that group of Pharisees just after we'd entered the city? They didn't look too happy about it.

Sarah	We always knew that they wouldn't understand. Well, they'll soon see. Once we get the people fully on our side . . .
Mark	Don't you think we ought to include Jesus in all of this planning?
Sarah	We will – when we've got a fully formed set of ideas to take to him.
Mark	It's just that he never does what we expect him to.
Sarah	But don't you see, Mark? Today – that was him finally declaring what he stands for. That was him making his stand. Saying to the Romans and the religious leaders, 'Look – here I am – and this is where the revolution begins.'
Mark	You think so?
Sarah	Absolutely. Political power . . . that's what we need. If you took half of that energy, that enthusiasm that was on the streets today . . . well, he had the people in the palm of his hand. They would have done anything for him.
Mark	But he didn't ask them, did he? I mean, with the crowd we had today we could have done something spectacular – but we turned around and came back out of the city again.
Sarah	You're right . . . but that's why Jesus needs us. We've got to show him how to take advantage of the situation, to get the people on his side and keep them there. He'll be fine.
Mark	I hope so. It's the only reason I joined this group.
Sarah	You and me both. But I'm sure he sees that. I'm sure he's got his eye on the main prize.
Mark	Well, you'd better be right. The people need a soldier who will lead a revolution not a street-corner preacher.
Sarah	And in Jesus they've got that. Today proves it . . . he's just been building up to this – biding his time . . . waiting to make his move.
Mark	Well, he couldn't have chosen a better time to do it.
Sarah	Exactly – or a better stage to do it on. It's going to be extraordinary. You mark my words – by the end of this week there's going to have been a revolution in this city and things are never going to be the same again.

6

Mothering Sunday

Mothering Sunday 1

The Plan

There is a laptop computer on a table – two people enter furtively and approach it. They are inept spies and act as if they might be discovered at any moment. No special costuming is necessary.

Spy 1	*(Looking around)* So, is he around?
Spy 2	Well, technically – since the being referred to is almighty God – gender doesn't come into it. We're talking about God here – 'he' could be a 'she' . . .
Spy 1	All right, all right. Let's just accept that it's convenient shorthand. Is he around?
Spy 2	Well, again, technically, since God is omnipresent, he's always around.
Spy 1	*(Getting exasperated)* We haven't got time for this. Can you see God?
Spy 2	Ah well, that's a metaphysical question . . .
Spy 1	Will you be quiet!
Spy 2	Sorry . . . and in answer to your question, no, he's not here at the moment, he's doing a spot of in-service training for archangels.
Spy 1	Good, then we can steal some of his design secrets. Let's see what he's been working on. *(Sits down at laptop and looks at screen)* Aha!
Spy 2	What is it?
Spy 1	I have no idea.
Spy 2	It looks like he's been working on something called 'a mother'.
Spy 1	Yes, but look. This has got to be wrong. According to this, mothers have eyes in the backs of their heads.

Spy 2	And the ability to get a two-year-old child to wash behind its ears . . . impossible.
Spy 1	Let's scroll down a bit more. *(Operates laptop)*
Spy 2	*(Reading)* Never-ending supply of love and hugs . . .
Spy 1	Ability to see through children's bedroom doors so that when she asks, 'What are you doing in there?' she already knows.
Spy 2	Six pairs of hands for binding scraped knees and cooking all at the same time.
Spy 1	This is ludicrous – he cannot be serious.
Spy 2	Ability to wipe crayon off bathroom tiles and keep smiling.
Spy 1	And look at this: tough enough to take the heartbreak that sometimes comes with raising children while also being soft enough to have a shoulder to cry on at all times of the day or night.
Spy 2	This is amazing. Look: the ability to care for sick children while feeling pretty rough herself.
Spy 1	And completely unselfish – putting the needs of her family above her own time and time again.
Spy 2	An ability to care for teenagers without going mad . . .
Spy 1	*(Looking up)* Oh, he's bitten off more than he can chew this time. Even God can't achieve this.
Spy 2	*(Reading screen)* Look, it leaks too.
Spy 1	That's not a leak, you fool, it's a tear. Tears of love and joy. Tears as the first child goes to school, at the broken heart of her teenager, at the graduation ceremony and the wedding.
Spy 2	This is amazing.
Spy 1	It's wonderful. Think how our lives would have been different if we'd had somebody like that.
Spy 2	*(Beginning to cry)* Mummy!
Spy 1	Look, we're never going to be able to duplicate this.
Spy 2	We could try.
Spy 1	What . . . and risk getting the whole thing terribly wrong? He doesn't even supply them with an instruction booklet.
Spy 2	No, I suppose that's why he's all powerful and we're idiots.
Spy 1	Exactly. Let's see if there's anything else in here we can nick . . . *(Looks at computer)*
Spy 2	*(Looking at screen)* Aha! TV celebrity chef . . . that should be a lot easier.

Mothering Sunday 2

Mother Church

Two actors stand centrally. This simple two-narrator piece should be delivered brightly and with energy. No special costuming is necessary.

Voice 1	The Church is like a mother to us.
Voice 2	A what?
Voice 1	A mother.
Voice 2	No, it's not, the church is that redbrick building on the housing estate.
Voice 1	It's also that rather grand but costly Victorian pile with a steeple down the road.
Voice 2	It's even that large building in the centre of town that used to be a cinema but is being used by the Pentecostals now.
Voice 1	It's also a humble mud-brick building in the middle of a remote village in Tanzania.
Voice 2	Yes, it's all those things – so it can't be a mother.
Voice 1	Why not?
Voice 2	Because it's got four walls and a door, that's why not. It's a building.
Voice 1	I'm not disputing the fact that it's a building.
Voice 2	Thank goodness for that – at least there's something we agree on.
Voice 1	Yes, there is. But it's more than just a building . . . it's a mother to us.
Voice 2	You're just trying to wind me up now, aren't you? Admit it, this is some elaborate plot to get me to lose my cool. That's it, isn't it? You're messing with my head.
Voice 1	Now, would I do that to you?
Voice 2	Yes.
Voice 1	I'm shocked that you'd even think that. Let's see if I can explain. Listen – what do you feel when you go to church?
Voice 2	Cold.
Voice 1	Now it's your turn to wind *me* up. Seriously, what do you feel?
Voice 2	I suppose I feel accepted, loved, supported, cared for.
Voice 1	Uh-huh.
Voice 2	What do you mean 'uh-huh'?

Voice 1	Well, isn't that exactly how a *mother* makes you feel?
Voice 2	*(Realizing)* Oh ... all right. So that's why the Church is like a mother to us. So, don't tell me, now you're going to get all superior and 'I told you so' about it, aren't you?
Voice 1	Not at all. Christians over hundreds of years have talked about 'mother Church' – about a building that's more than a building. An institution that's more than an institution. At its best it has loved us when we have been unlovable ...
Voice 2	Cared for us when we have strayed ...
Voice 1	Always been there for us even though we sometimes haven't cared.
Voice 2	Wherever you go in the world, it's there.
Voice 1	With doors open wide in acceptance and love.
Voice 2	It's a deep relationship of trust and love.
Voice 1	And as long as Christ is at the centre of the Church then it's a relationship that will never let us go and will grow and develop over the years.
Voice 2	It's rather a nice picture, isn't it?
Voice 1	Yes, it is. And on a day like today it's a very helpful picture as well.
Voice 2	Why's that then?
Voice 1	Well, it's Mothering Sunday.
Voice 2	What? Why didn't you tell me? A card, chocolates, flowers, I've done nothing! *(Runs off)*
Voice 1	Oh. Sorry about that. Anyway, to sum up, the Church is like a mother to us, and that ... unlike my friend ... can be depended upon.

7

Easter

Easter Day Year A

Acts 10.34–43   John 20.1–18

Everyone   *Acts 10.34–43*
Jane and Chloe enter looking at an invitation card. They are bright and cheerful if a little narrow minded. No special costuming is necessary.

Jane	It's for everyone – that's the difficult bit.
Chloe	Are you sure? Because that's going to lead to all sorts of problems.
Jane	It is, isn't it? I mean, even with my catering skills the sausages on sticks won't go round that many people.
Chloe	No, it's more than that – because if this is right – if it really is for everyone, then that means we're going to have to open this up to people we don't like very much, and I'm not really sure I want to do that.
Jane	We'll have to welcome that man with the bad breath.
Chloe	And that old woman from round the corner with the big teeth.
Jane	And that family from number 46 with the uncontrollable children.

There is silence while they both contemplate this.

Chloe	Do you really think they mean everybody? Because if they do, where do you stop? What about the people who hang around the town centre?
Jane	Or the travellers from the campsite?
Chloe	Our little meetings have always been so nice up until now.
Jane	Well, that's because they've been made up of people like us.
Chloe	Who think like us . . .

Jane	Talk like us . . .
Chloe	Well, actually . . . us.
Jane	It's been nice with just the two of us really, hasn't it?
Chloe	Very nice indeed.
Jane	But it does clearly say 'everyone'. *(Looking at the card and reading)* I died for all and rose for all. Invite everybody.
Chloe	It does sound rather exciting.
Jane	If not a little bit scary.
Chloe	Do you think other people will come?
Jane	Well, I suppose that's their decision. But if we've never asked, how will we ever know?
Chloe	It is an absolutely amazing thought that this is for absolutely everyone, isn't it?
Jane	The whole of humanity – past, present and still to come.
Chloe	Every background, every colour and creed. Everyone.
Jane	Everyone.
Chloe	We've got very good at counting people out, Jane.
Jane	I think it's time we started counting them in.
Chloe	I think we might have to get in a few more cocktail sticks!

Peter remembers   *John 20.1–18*

This dramatic monologue imagines the words of Peter. He is impetuous, emotional and open-hearted. No special costuming is necessary.

Every time I remember that glorious day the excitement and wonder come flooding back. I've never been a man who's good with words. I feel a lot . . . too much sometimes. I'm forever putting my foot in my mouth. But ask me to find the words to describe what went on that day . . . well I've been asked time and time again, as you can imagine. People are always coming up to me and saying, 'Peter, what was it like? How did you feel? Take us through that day, Peter.' Well, I try my best – but I'm never satisfied. I never do it justice. I just can't find the words.

You've got to remember that the previous couple of days . . . well, to say they'd been difficult would be an understatement. I didn't think it was humanly possible to sink as low as we had done. The supper, the trial, and then that horrible death. To stand by and watch and be so helpless – not to have been able to do a thing to stop it. And, of course, I'd denied that I even knew him. That was the worst part of all. To have come so far . . . to have loved him so much and to be able to stand there and to say that I didn't even know him. It was more than I could take.

I don't remember much of Saturday at all. It's hazy – like a half-remembered nightmare that you've managed to block from your mind. And then came Sunday. We woke but we had no plan . . . no sense of where the day was going to lead. Should we split up and go our separate ways? Start the journey back to our families? It wasn't as if they wouldn't be pleased to see us. I'd been away for the best part of three years. Yes – it was a question that was on everybody's mind. There just wasn't anybody there who was brave enough to ask it.

It was still dark when Mary came bursting in. Half terrified, half excited – her eyes wide with what she'd seen. It took a while to calm her down and when we did, the words she said made no sense. She said that they'd moved the body. The stone had been rolled away from the entrance to the tomb. Well, John and I couldn't believe it. Why on earth would they want to do that? Move the body . . . why? We raced through the dawn light to the tomb. We got there to find it just as Mary had said. The stone that had blocked the tomb entrance was standing to one side and there was the entrance to the tomb. John had stopped but I pushed past him into the tomb. I had to know – I had to know for certain – to see with my own eyes. And as I did that the threads of some of the things that Jesus said began to work their way through my mind. 'Three days,' he had said. 'Three days.' I looked in – hardly daring to hope – and there I saw the linen wrappings lying there as if nobody had any use of them anymore. And the cloth that had been round his head – there it was rolled up by the side.

John and I looked at each other – and you have never known so much said without words. What if all he'd said – all he'd prophesied – was true?

This was going to be just the beginning.

Easter Day Year B

1 Corinthians 15.1–11   Mark 16.1–8

Passing on   *1 Corinthians 15.1–11*
This dramatic meditative piece explores the idea of passing on the gospel message. It should be delivered warmly, gently and with feeling. No special costuming is necessary.

'Here it is,' she said, and held out to me a small parcel. There was a world of meaning in that holding out and giving. You could tell. You just knew from every movement of her body how precious this was. The gentle, careful way in which she held the parcel, the fondness in her expression, the slow, infinitely tender way in which she picked it up and offered it. I hardly dared to take it from her. It was quite obvious that this was extraordinarily important to her – that her being was somehow connected to what was inside.

'I can't take this from you.' I said. Who was I to take something that clearly meant so much to her? I couldn't do it – couldn't deprive her of what gave her such hope and joy.

She seemed to read my thoughts.

'But I have to give it to you,' she said, smiling, 'it's my duty to pass it on. It always has been. And don't think you're depriving me of anything by taking it. It renews itself in the giving. Now that I have it, nobody can take it away from me. But it's given me such joy . . . it's brought me such hope and meaning and purpose. I don't know how I could have lived without it. After that . . . not to offer it, not to pass it on to somebody else so that they too can discover what I have discovered – not to do that seems like the ultimate act of selfishness and greed. I can't do that. I just can't. So I offer it to you. I pass it on. And once you've experienced – once you know – you'll want to pass it on too.'

And so she gave it to me. And she was right. There is nothing more important in my life than passing this on – nothing that will bring me more joy – a greater sense of being complete – than the act of sharing this with you. And so I do what hundreds – thousands – of people before me have done . . . I pass it on.

Not here   *Mark 16.1–8*

This two-narrator piece is about the importance of Christians being in the world. One can be standing centrally as Two enters from the audience/congregation. Two is anxious and slightly nervous. One is more assured. No special costuming is necessary.

One	He's not here.
Two	Isn't he?
One	No – he's already gone.
Two	Oh . . . okay. Where's he gone?
One	Out there. *(Points outwards)*
Two	Out where?
One	Out there where people are living their lives. He's gone out there to be with them, challenge them, bring them hope and joy and life.
Two	Oh . . . *(pause)* I'll wait here then, shall I?
One	Why don't you go out there to be with him?

Two	*(Looks unsure)* I don't know – it all looks a bit threatening . . . a bit uncertain.
One	It'll be fine. All you need is a bit of courage.
Two	Yes . . . hmm . . . courage . . . never my strongest suit.
One	He's always doing the unexpected, isn't he?
Two	You're right there.
One	Never where you expect him to be.
Two	Never.
One	You expected him to be here, didn't you?
Two	Well, I did watch him die. I did see them put his body in the tomb. Since he was dead it only stood to reason that he would still be here.
One	Inconvenient, isn't it?
Two	A little bit, yes.
One	He did tell you that death was not the end.
Two	I thought he was speaking metaphorically.
One	Ah . . . well, I think you ought to go out there to be with him.
Two	Do you?
One	It's clearly where he wants you to be. Sharing his work . . .
Two	Yes . . .
One	Sharing in the joy of new life.
Two	*(Beginning to warm to the idea)* It is quite exciting, isn't it?
One	That's the idea.
Two	New life . . . death defeated . . . wonderful.
One	Quite right.
Two	And he's out there, you say?
One	Out in the world he created.
Two	Doing something extraordinary no doubt.
One	No doubt.
Two	And wanting me to join him.
One	Absolutely.
Two	Then I'm going!
One	Excellent – he'll be overjoyed to see you.
Two	Off I go.
One	Wait a minute . . .
Two	What?
One	I'm coming with you!
They exit.	

Easter Day Year C

1 Corinthians 15.19–26   Luke 24.1–12

Could you explain?   *1 Corinthians 15.19–26*

This piece only needs two people even though more are implied. Maddy needs to be at a table or desk. She is bright and enthusiastic – always eager to take part. Her dress can emphasize her role (such as an old school tie and messy hair). The teacher is slightly world-weary and stands in front of a class with a Bible – they read . . .

Teacher	'As in Adam, all men die, so in Christ all will be brought to life.'

Maddy has her hand up.

Maddy	Sir, sir, sir, please sir!
Teacher	*(With a tiredness born of long suffering)* Yes, Maddy, what is it now?
Maddy	What about the women, sir?
Teacher	I beg your pardon?
Maddy	Well, you just said, 'As in Adam, all *men* die.' Does that mean only men die, sir? What about the women, sir? Did Eve not die, sir? Are women not included in the divine plan of salvation, sir?
Teacher	Of course, they're included, Maddy – the use of the word 'men' here isn't meant to count anybody out.
Maddy	Oh that's good, sir, because it sounded like it was.
Teacher	Absolutely not. Now, if we can continue. . .
Maddy	Oh, yes, sir, of course, sir. Carry on, sir.
Teacher	So, as I was saying . . .
Maddy	Sir?
Teacher	Yes, Maddy?
Maddy	Can I just check that I understand it all?
Teacher	Of course.
Maddy	So . . . if I've got it right . . . Adam was disobedient . . . he ate the fruit that he'd been told not to eat and that's when he discovered he'd got no clothes on. *(She sniggers)*
Teacher	That's right.
Maddy	So he disobeyed God and humans have been disobeying God ever since. That sounds like our relationship, doesn't it sir? Because I disobey you all the time, don't I?

Teacher	Yes, Maddy, but I'm hardly God am I?
Maddy	I suppose not, sir. Anyway – that meant Jesus had to come – because he was going to be obedient to God, beat death and be raised from the dead so that we can have a fantastic friendship with God.
Teacher	*(Slightly surprised that Maddy has grasped the point)* Actually, that's exactly right, Maddy, well done. Well done indeed.
Maddy	Thank you, sir. *(She ponders)* Sir?
Teacher	Yes, Maddy?
Maddy	It changes everything, doesn't it?
Teacher	What do you mean?
Maddy	Well, Easter Day, the resurrection and all that . . . it changes absolutely everything.
Teacher	It does, Maddy . . . it really does.
Maddy	Wow.

They exit.

Joanna remembers   *Luke 24.1–12*

This dramatic monologue gives voice to the thoughts of a lesser-known biblical character who is happy to play a supporting role. No special costuming is necessary.

I was certainly not what anybody would ever call a natural witness. I'm not famous, not well known – Luke only mentions me twice and each time it's a throwaway comment. The first time he even defines me by who I was married to!

I was never going to make a mark. My parents told me as much. 'You'll never amount to anything,' my mother used to say. It was the same in the village where we lived. Nobody ever paid any attention to anything I had to say. It was almost as if I was invisible – completely passed by – bland little Joanna sitting in the corner. I was the very definition of ordinary. You know how you're likely to remember the really bright or the really naughty? I was neither, and I sort of disappeared. Now there are lots of people who think that that must have been a terrible thing. They assume that I hated being ordinary. They believe that I must have spent most of my time longing to break out in some way . . . be noticed. That kind of person is always really disappointed when they find out that I was actually really very happy. I never wanted to stand out. I was absolutely desperate to keep out of the spotlight. Let other people take centre stage. I was more than content not drawing attention to myself at every opportunity.

I cannot describe to you how terrible that Friday was. Standing there helplessly watching life ebb slowly from him. All we could do was hold each other and weep. I still find it hard to talk about it. *(Pause)* I'm sorry.

So then on the Sunday morning we took the spices that we'd prepared down to the tomb. I'm not sure what we thought we were going to find. After all, the body was in the cave, the rock had been rolled over the entrance. I don't know how we thought we were going to get access to anything. But we were going mad with grief – we had to get out, do something, at least feel as though we had the possibility of being useful.

The rest you know. And suddenly I was thrown into the role of being a witness. I was one of the first witnesses as it turns out – me, ordinary, quiet, shy, tongue-tied Joanna who normally avoided attention as if my life depended on it – suddenly being the first witness to the greatest event in the history of the world. I always said that God had a strange and warped sense of humour. And of course if I can do it – if an ordinary, everyday person like me can do it – then anybody can. Which means, of course, that you can too.

8

Pentecost

Pentecost Year A

1 Corinthians 12.3b–13   Acts 2.1–21

Ralph and Jim on variety   *1 Corinthians 12.3b–13*
Ralph is sitting centrally, Jim enters. Ralph and Jim are talking heads who enjoy sharing their general ignorance over a pint. No special costuming is necessary but a table and chairs are needed.

Jim	Wotcha, Ralph mate. How's it going?
Ralph	As it goes, Jim, it's going pretty well. How's it going with you?
Jim	Can't complain, Ralphy boy, can't complain. Actually, I've been doing a bit of thinking.
Ralph	Thinking, Jim? Steady on . . . you want to be careful about that – you never know what's going to happen.
Jim	I know, Ralph mate, I know, but I can't help it. I can't stop thinking bout . . . variety.
Ralph	What, like Saturday-night variety? You know I love that Bruce Forsyth, mate, he's a singing, dancing, joke-telling superstar . . . that's what he is.
Jim	No, not like Saturday variety.
Ralph	Oh . . . shame, 'cos the only thing better than Bruce Forsyth is Des O'Connor, mate – now there's a variety phenomenon.
Jim	That's not the kind of variety I was thinking about.
Ralph	So what were you thinking about then?
Jim	I was thinking about the fact that variety is built into the beating heart of the universe – that's what I was thinking.
Ralph	*(Pause)* You what?
Jim	Look, Ralph mate – look around you. There is wonderful variety everywhere you care to take a gander. Not just one kind of flower

but millions, thousands of different butterflies, birds, fish . . . it's everywhere.

Ralph   Oh . . .

Jim   And don't even get me started on people – we're the most varied of the lot. Some are loud, others are quiet. Some are great at seeing the big picture, others are into the details. Some are good at solving problems, others are good at causing them.

Ralph   It is amazing when you think about it, Jim mate.

Jim   It certainly is Ralph, and it all comes from one place, dunnit?

Ralph   What do you mean, Jim?

Jim   God, mate, God. The Supreme Being, the Creator whose spirit is everywhere breathing life into us, making us varied, giving each one of us a different set of gifts and abilities.

Ralph   You know, Jim, my Gran was brilliant at crosswords, loved practical jokes and could play the tuba.

Jim   Exactly – my Uncle Jack was a really quiet guy who hated crowds but used to go around on his bike visiting the old folks – he was 86.

Ralph   We've all got different gifts . . . you, Jim mate, are really good at praying.

Jim   Oh, thank you, Ralphy – you're fantastic at encouraging people.

Ralph   Just as well we're all so different – it would be really boring if we were the same.

Jim   All gifts from one Spirit, Ralph mate . . . what glorious, God-given, variety.

This sketch was first published in ROOTS, © ROOTS for Churches Ltd, www.rootsontheweb.com, reproduced with permission

A bystander remembers   *Acts 2.1–21*

This dramatic monologue imagines the spoken thoughts of a member of the crowd on the day of Pentecost. He or she is warm and chatty. No special costuming is necessary.

When people ask me about it, they always assume that I'm going to say that it was the dramatic events of that day that most stick in my mind. One minute we were just making our way through the city as best we could on a very busy day. The next minute these wild men, their arms flailing, rush into the crowd and start speaking ten to the dozen. And it *was* memorable, and intense, and slightly scary. But actually that's not the thing that I remember most about that day. What I remember, if you really want to know, is the sermon.

Yes, I know, I know. Whoever remembers sermons? They're things to doze during, daydream through – not things to remember with complete clarity as though it happened yesterday. And it didn't have the most promising of starts. There was jeering from a certain section of the crowd that had gathered. A couple of local comedians were calling out that these guys were probably drunk.

I will always remember what happened next. One of the group – I later found out his name was Peter – stepped forward and began to speak. He was medium height but thick-set and rugged . . . a working man. His hands were cracked and covered in nicks and scratches. His face was weathered and tanned from having spent most of his life outdoors. This Peter looked around at us and began to speak. I will never forget it. He spoke with a strong accent but the words were so passionate, so full of truth. He managed not only to convince us that *he* believed the words he was saying to us, but that we should believe them too.

It was the most powerful thing I have ever seen – this ordinary working man talking to us about the love and the plans of God. He talked about an outpouring of the love of God, and by the time he had finished not one of us there doubted that that love had been poured out on all of us that day.

I left the square knowing that everything had changed, that something quite extraordinary had happened. I did not pretend that I knew what God was going to do next but I felt a presence . . . a power that I had never felt before. In whatever way it had happened – and I didn't even want to try and explain it – I knew that God had come to us that day.

Pentecost Year B

Ezekiel 37.1–14 (see Fifth Sunday in Lent Year A, p. 112)
   John 15.26–27;16.4b–15   Acts 2.1–21

The judge   *John 15.26–7; 16.4b–15*
Two actors stand centrally – one is on trial, the other is the Spirit. This should be delivered with serious conviction. If you can supply a dock for the 'The World' (perhaps a lectern or pulpit), that would be good. A gown for the Spirit to wear would also be helpful.

Spirit   *(Addressing the congregation/audience)* Now then, ladies and gentlemen, welcome to the court. We are here today to accuse 'The World' of the most serious crimes.

World	Wait a minute, I'm not sure I recognize the legality of these proceedings. Who are you again?
Spirit	I am the Advocate, and I come in judgement – and these are the courts of God.
World	Wait a minute . . . the Advocate? Isn't that another name for the Holy Spirit?
Spirit	That is correct.
World	But aren't you meant to be all warm and fuzzy?
Spirit	Have you read your scriptures?
World	Well, not as often as I'd like to, no. I've had other things on my mind, like smartphones and computer games.
Spirit	Then you wouldn't have noticed that I'm called the Advocate for a reason – it's a legal term . . . one that implies judgement.
World	Well, that's a bit harsh . . . I mean come on.
Spirit	Tell me . . . World . . . the Son of God was sent to you and what happened while he was in the World?
World	*(Pause)* He was killed.
Spirit	That is quite correct . . . to be exact he was crucified . . . isn't that right, World?
World	Well, yes.
Spirit	And the people who tried and convicted Jesus accused him of sin, did they not?
World	I suppose . . .
Spirit	There's no supposing about it. And is it not correct, World, that for the next 2,000 years humanity often used God as an excuse to justify its own prejudice, hatred and violence?
World	Possibly.
Spirit	I submit that the inhabitants of the World have used God as an excuse to murder, maim and destroy for hundreds of years. And that you have consistently ignored the teachings and the significance of the Prince of Peace.
World	Well, that's hardly my fault . . . he was so different from anything I expected.
Spirit	And your expectations were wrong, weren't they?
World	As it turns out . . . yes. But you could have given me a bit of warning that he was going to be so different.
Spirit	You were given ample warning – you just chose to ignore it as you always do. And now I have been sent as Advocate. Let the trial begin . . .

Birthday   *Acts 2.1–21*

An angel sits centrally – Roberta is full of good down-to-earth common sense. No special costuming should be used.

Hello everybody, good morning, how are you all? My name's Roberta, and you might not be able to tell this just by looking at me, but I am an angel. Yes I know, I know – I don't look all that angelic. I get that a lot. Well, let me tell you, us angels come in all kinds of shapes and sizes.

I need to be honest with you straight away. I'm actually still quite new to this angel lark. I haven't got my wings yet. In fact I've only just recently graduated from BATS – that's Basic Angel Training School for those of you who aren't up on 'angel lingo'. Top of my class I'll have you know.

Anyway – that's not what I've come to talk to you about today. The fact is that I wanted a word with you all about spiritual matters – yes. In fact 'Holy' spiritual matters – and today being Pentecost seemed an ideal time for that.

You know, I have to tell you that there seems to be very little that gets you Christians more riled with each other than conversation about the Holy Spirit. Talk about angels dancing on the heads of pins (which by the way we don't do very often you know) – you seem to want to spend all your time and energy defining a mystery . . . putting walls up around the divine. Now why would you want to do that is what I want to know? Why can you not just relax and revel in the glorious generosity of God?

I know I haven't been an angel very long, but it seems to me that all of this time and energy you spend tiring yourselves out with discussions about who the Spirit is and what the Spirit does – well that time and energy could be more usefully spent asking God to allow you to open yourself up and enjoy all the gifts of the Spirit that God wants to give you. After all, Pentecost has often been called the birthday of the Church hasn't it? So why don't you just relax and allow God to give you a birthday present?

Go on.

Pentecost Year C

Genesis 11.1–9   Acts 2.1–21

Language problem   *Genesis 11.1–9*

A newsreader sits at a desk. Aaron is smart, slightly self-important and pompous. If a suitable news-theme tune can be played as introduction, so much the better.

Aaron	Good morning, I am Aaron Hardhitter, and this is the Old Testament news. This just in. We are getting unconfirmed reports of construction chaos in the city centre where building seems to have come to a complete standstill on the latest highrise development. Viewers will know that in the heart of the city work has been moving forward for some time now on a really tall tower . . . called 'the really tall tower project'. This giant structure has been growing by leaps and bounds. Billed by its architects as a 'stairway to the heavens', the structure is already massively over budget and now seems to have been plagued by even more trouble. To find out what's happening we're going to go live to foreman of construction on the project, Mitch Harding. So, Mitch, what seems to be the problem?

Mitch enters and stands to one side

Mitch	Well, Aaron, I'm not quite sure what to say . . . in all of my professional career nothing like this has ever happened. *(Pause)* By the way . . . can you understand what I'm saying to you?
Aaron	Absolutely, Mitch – there's no problem at all.
Mitch	Well, that's a relief . . . because down here nobody can understand a word I'm saying.
Aaron	And why would that be?
Mitch	Well, you know, Aaron, I have no idea. All I know is that when I went to bed last night everybody was using the same language as each other, and this morning when I got up everybody was talking gibberish. I really have no clue as to what's going on . . . literally. I talked to our architect this morning, and I didn't understand a word of what he told me.
Aaron	Well, Mitch, that's going to make continued work on 'the really tall tower project' almost impossible, isn't it?
Mitch	We've had to shut everything down – and I think we've got the health and safety people coming down this morning, although whether we'll be able to understand what they tell us when they get here is anybody's guess.
Aaron	Well, thanks so much for being with us, Mitch.
Mitch	That's no problem – to be honest it's quite a relief to find somebody who understands what I'm saying.
Aaron	Well, folks, you heard it here first. That is, of course, if you can understand the words I'm using. Does language unite us or divide

us? And has God got some part to play in our understanding of each other? We'll be following up these and other questions as our programme continues. After the break we'll be looking at vanity building projects and asking, 'Have we got too big for our boots?' We'll be right back.

Just what we need   Acts 2.1–21

A member of the temple hierarchy enters in character. He/she is self-important and slightly frustrated at the inconvenience of everything that has taken place. No special costuming is necessary.

I have to say, I thought all of this was over . . . but apparently not. I thought we'd neatly wrapped up all the loose ends. We'd sorted the crucifixion. We'd weathered the next few difficult days – including the slightly unfortunate situation at the tomb on the Sunday morning. Just as an aside I have to say that you cannot get good-quality troops anymore. All they had to do was guard a dead body . . . it really can't be that difficult can it? But what do I know?

Anyway, we seemed to have come out the other side of that unscathed. Even though the body had disappeared, to my complete surprise it did not seem like we were going to need it anyway. For a month things had been very quiet. His followers had gone to ground. I was hearing nothing about anything to do with the empty tomb, and I was just about to breathe a rather large sigh of relief. It seemed that the name Jesus was going to disappear, thank goodness.

Then this morning happened. There'd been no sign of it beforehand. No sign or signal that anything was wrong. I should know – I've had one of my best men tracking the disciples for days now. He was under strict instructions to report back to me should there be anything suspicious at all, and I'd heard nothing. That is until today. It seems that it all started early this morning when the main group of them burst out of the house that they'd been holed up in, jabbering excitedly. And it really was jabbering as I understand it. My man could hardly understand a word that was being said – although the crowd seemed to lap it up – appealing to the masses again.

Then, Peter – that hot-headed, difficult fisherman – stands up in front of the crowd and speaks in the most miraculous – the most extraordinary – way. He talks of Jesus and what has happened and begs people to understand. My spy tells me that he is quite transformed from the man he was a few days ago. Fearless – and apparently he has a way with words that he didn't have before. Quite the public speaker . . . we're going to have to keep a good watch on him.

So, just as I thought it was all over, it starts up again. But with Jesus gone I don't think they're going to be anything like the threat that they were. Even Peter with his new-found skills in public speaking is no match for the pressure I can bring to bear. No – trust me – you've heard the last that you're going to hear of Jesus.

9

Trinity Sunday

Trinity Sunday Year A

Genesis 1.1 — 2.4a   Matthew 28.16–20

Relationship   *Genesis 1.1 — 2.4a*
This dramatic meditation should be delivered with enthusiasm and a real sense of wonder.

'The most exciting thing about it – the most glorious thing is that it's dynamic,' she said, her eyes twinkling with the wonder of it. She sat back in her easy chair and fixed her gaze on the young boy who sat eagerly taking in her every word.

'Dynamic?' he asked.

She laughed and stretched out her arms, 'Have you ever tried to describe God?' she asked. He had to admit that he didn't think so. 'Well, let me tell you, it isn't easy. In fact it's probably about the most difficult thing you could ever try to do.

'God, you know, well, he, she or it is such a big idea. The power, the love, the forgiveness, the grace, the peace, the justice . . . well, you get the idea. It's a pretty big thing to get your head around. Those people who claim that they've done it . . . that they understand God fully – well, they're just lying. I'm sorry, but I don't believe them. But we're humans, and being human we've always wanted to try to put into words what we can't describe. It's just the way we're made. But how do you describe the indescribable? How do you even begin to try to explain who or what God is? Well, one way to do it is to recognize that at the heart of God is a dynamic relationship of love.'

'There is?' he asked . . . wide-eyed.

'Absolutely. That's why creation is so glorious and endlessly fascinating. It reflects the heart of God, which is a dynamic thing. Just look at the world – mountain tops and butterflies, coral reefs and hummingbirds – it is quite extraordinary in its richness and variety. How can you use language to describe a God that great, that powerful? You talk about relationship at the heart of it all. A creative relationship of love that spills out into the entire universe – that's what God is and what God does. It is breathtaking in its risk and dynamism and love.'

She looked at the young boy and smiled. He had understood some of what she had tried to say but not all of it. She hadn't expected him to. She did not understand all of it herself. But the journey of exploration was an immense adventure and she had enjoyed every minute of it.

A missionary God   Matthew 28.16–20

Two church members sit centrally. Both characters are keen to witness but are completely defeated by the obstacles they face. No special costuming is necessary.

One	So, let's get down to some serious planning for our mission here at St Thomas the Doubtful.
Two	Yes, let's.
One	Now, we're going to have a walk of witness through the town centre.
Two	Ah . . .
One	What do you mean 'ah'?
Two	Well, I've contacted the Police and they've sent me a 15-page risk-assessment form to fill in . . . here it is. *(Waves form)*
One	That sounds a bit complicated.
Two	It is. They want uniformed marshals every fifteen metres, water stations and no singing.
One	No singing?
Two	They say it would break the noise abatement order on the town centre.
One	Oh. Well, perhaps we'd better cancel that then. Well – no matter – let's move on to our next exciting event. The leaflet drop across the town.
Two	Ah . . .
One	There it is again.
Two	Nobody wanted to do it.
One	Why ever not?
Two	Well, they didn't like the fluorescent yellow jackets they were going to have to wear, nobody wanted to do their own street

	and the nights are drawing in and nobody wanted to do it in the dark.
One	Good grief. Well, at least we've still got the ecumenical open-air praise event.
Two	Ah . . .
One	Not again. What now?
Two	Well, none of the churches could decide where it should be. The Methodists wanted it in the supermarket car park, the Catholics wanted it outside the school, and we said we wanted it in the park.
One	And nobody would compromise?
Two	Absolutely not . . . it's a matter of principle.
One	So we don't have the walk of witness, the leaflet drop or the ecumenical praise event . . . what do we have?
Two	Well, I can tell you what we don't have.
One	What's that?
Two	Any money.
One	What!?
Two	I'm afraid the finance committee said that mission was too expensive, and they didn't vote us a budget.
One	They do understand that our God is a missionary God, don't they?
Two	They said they'd refer that question to a sub-committee and get back to us in six months' time.

Trinity Sunday Year B

Isaiah 6.1–8   Romans 8.12–17   John 3.1–17 (see Second Sunday in Lent Year A, p. 89)

Seeing   *Isaiah 6.1–8*
This meditation/poem could be read by two or more voices.

Awesome in splendour
High and lifted up
Exalted in majesty.
Before we become too familiar

Too comfortable
In the way we talk of the creator
It is worth remembering the God that Isaiah bowed down to.
A God whose robe filled the temple
And whom six winged angels ceaselessly praised.
This was a God who inspired awestruck wonder
Who was great in power
Glorious in might.
The heaven-built temple shook at God's words.
This house of worship was filled with smoke.
The only response was to fall down in worship
To call out in wonder and to realize your size –
How small, how tiny, how completely insignificant when compared . . .
with this God who was called:
Holy, holy, holy!
Perhaps before we fall to the temptation to make God our size
It might be good to remember who it is we worship,
And that we need to tread carefully when we stand on holy ground.
To God be the glory
And the wonder
And the praise for ever
Amen.
And again I say, Amen!

Doing good   Romans 8.12–17

A market trader enters from the back. The trader is loud and never short of a comment. The customer is interested but wary. No special costuming is necessary.

Trader	Come on then, come on everybody. Come and have a look – I've got your genuine Christian qualities for sale here just for today. They're going to go quickly so get some while they're still here.
Customer	*(Entering)* Christian qualities for sale?
Trader	Absolutely, come and have a look, don't be shy. Each and every one a bargain.
Customer	So what about this one?
Trader	Ah, and a very good choice if you don't mind my saying so. That is your genuine persistence in prayer that is. Guaranteed to help you keep on praying even on days when it seems difficult.
Customer	I see, and this?

Trader	Ah, our best seller that one. That's calling down blessings on your persecutors not curses. Very useful . . . very useful indeed. I mean, how many of us actually feel like being pleasant to people that make our lives a misery, eh? Be honest . . . not very many of us. And that's why you need one of these.
Customer	I see – what else have you got?
Trader	Ah, well, I've got: hope to keep you joyful, giving to the needs of others, hospitality, a special-caring-for-others pack, never paying back evil for evil, living at peace with everybody, and the ever-popular feeding-and-giving-a-drink-to-your-enemy.
Customer	I see – when you list everything like that it makes the Christian life sound pretty difficult, doesn't it?
Trader	Ah, well, you see that's why you need to get these Christian qualities from me. That way you'll never have a problem.
Customer	But I thought God was meant to help with all of this?
Trader	I beg your pardon?
Customer	I thought that was why belief in the Trinity was so important. Belief in the creator God who sends Jesus into the world and then pours down the Spirit to enable, strengthen and guide us.
Trader	Well, if you're going to bring God into it . . .
Customer	But surely that's the whole point of living a Christian life? God IS in it by default really. Surely we need God's help even to come close to living a good life?
Trader	But it's so much easier to buy the life from me.
Customer	I'm not sure it's meant to be easy.
Trader	Look, all I'm trying to do is make a living by selling people a lifestyle.
Customer	I'm not sure this lifestyle can be bought.
Trader	Look, off with you . . . go on. Coming in here and mucking up my sales pitch. I'll have you know I've been fleecing people for years, and I've never had a complaint . . . course that might be 'cos people actually want to be fleeced. If they want the easy way to a satisfying life, I'll sell 'em something that looks just like the real thing. Now get going. *They exit.*

Trinity Sunday Year C

Proverbs 8.1–4, 22–31   John 16.12–15

The Spirit speaks   *Proverbs 8.1–4, 22–31*
This dramatic meditation should be delivered with a sense of awe-inspired wonder and barely concealed excitement.

I'm telling you, if you had only been there.

It was glorious – to be there as the skies slowly formed, as the first clouds billowed. I watched as mountains rose, as rivers first made their way bubbling across the new-formed land to the ocean, as the foundations of earth knit together. It was magnificent.

There was delight all the time. To play in that creation . . . to splash in newborn streams, to take flight on the back of a huge bird as it soared into a newly minted sky. I used to plunge down deep into the depths of the oceans to see the wonders that were found there. I would bounce along on the backs of unnamed animals, clinging to, the new-made fur. It was wonderful. The laughter-making, awe-inspiring, glorious delight of it all – it was . . . fantastic.

And at the heart of it all was a relationship of dynamic, divine love that burst out of every pore and newly formed canyon and cave. Love was everywhere. We saw the world as it came into being and we danced with delight.

If only you could see what relationship is capable of, your breath would catch in your throat. We are a community of love, but too often you do not see that. We are three in one, and all too often you want to live and work alone. You do not see what can come from co-operation, you do not accept that it is good to share.

I wish I could show you what wisdom can achieve. I wish I could help you to see. But now it is all small hand-held screens and shopping malls. Now it is all about how quickly a journey can be made or a task done. It is all I can do to encourage you to look up from your tiny screen long enough to look at the world around you. You have developed so much cleverness and so little wisdom.

But there is hope. Every time I see a child gaze in wonder at a lion, every time I watch as a person is spellbound as they encounter a glorious view, I smile.

We toiled in creation to make something breathtaking, and when you recognize, if only for a moment, the splendour of what is around you . . . well, it makes us dance with delight all over again.

Guided into truth   *John 16.12–15*

Two actors stand centrally. This simple two-narrator piece needs to be delivered with energy and pace. No special costuming is necessary.

One	I like the idea of being guided.
Two	Because sometimes I have no idea where I am.
One	Thank goodness somebody feels the same way.
Two	The world is so confusing.
One	Scientific breakthroughs happen every other day it seems.
Two	And if that wasn't enough there are the moral questions . . .
One	The ethical dilemmas.
Two	What to say?
One	What to believe?
Two	How to respond?
One	It's confusing.
Two	Deeply puzzling.
One	I want to follow God.
Two	To be true to my Christian beliefs.
One	I might even be prepared to take a stand.
Two	*(To One)* That's daring of you.
One	I know . . . I even surprise myself sometimes. Yes . . . take a stand.
Two	If only I knew what stand to take.
One	And how . . .
Two	And when!
One	You see how difficult it is?
Two	Being faithful in a world that is moving so fast.
One	Standing up for value and dignity.
Two	In shifting sand.
One	So I am glad that we're promised a guide.
Two	A Spirit who is truth.
One	Who will lead us into God's truth.
Two	Of course, there are all kinds of questions about that.
One	I can think of one or two right now.
Two	Like how do you know the guidance is from God and not yourself?
One	How do you even get hold of this guidance in the first place?
Two	Yes . . . there are questions.

One	But . . .
Two	And it is a big 'but' . . .
One	If we wait quietly and humbly.
Two	Keeping ourselves open to the gentle promptings of the divine.
One	If we keep ourselves close to God.
Two	Studying the scriptures . . .
One	Constant in prayer . . .
Two	Then we will be guided into God's truth.
One	Slowly and carefully.
Two	With patience and wisdom.
One	And the truth that we will discover . . .
Two	Will set us free.

10

Harvest

Harvest 1

Dahlias and weeds   *1 Timothy 6.6–10*

Two actors walk to the front. No special costuming is necessary. Actor 1 is certain of her or his own brilliance; Actor 2 is humble and slightly nervous.

Actor 1	*(Big and expansive)* Welcome to Harvest Festival. I am a glorious dahlia!
Actor 2	*(Rather shamefaced)* And I'm a little weed.
Actor 1	See, everybody, look at my glorious colour, my wonderful petals.
Actor 2	I'm a dandelion, and I'm yellow.
Actor 1	I know I'm slightly difficult to grow, but look at how beautiful I am.
Actor 2	I get everywhere, I do. In your lawn, between cracks in the pavement, in your guttering . . . sorry about that. I'm very persistent.
Actor 1	Yes, persistence is one thing, but who would want to put you in a harvest display? I mean, why are you even here? I'm rare and slightly fragile, difficult to grow but with a blaze of colour.
Actor 2	Yes, I can see that. You're very beautiful.
Actor 1	And you, on the other hand . . . well, look at you. You're tough as old boots. What happened the last time somebody tried to dig you up?
Actor 2	I just came right on back.
Actor 1	Exactly – do you have any idea how frustrating you are? How difficult your roots are to dig up?
Actor 2	*(Chuckling)* I am a little obstinate.
Actor 1	Obstinate? Obstinate? That's putting it mildly. Just when gardeners think they've dug deep enough, that they've managed to clear out the whole of your root system . . .

Actor 2	I go and prove them wrong. I'm tough that way.
Actor 1	I'm so special and you're so ordinary.
Actor 2	Yes, I know.
Actor 1	So do you really think you ought to be here at all? In this harvest display?
Actor 2	Well, I'm not sure – but the preacher said I had pride of place.
Actor 1	What? How dare she! Pride of place? What an affront! I've never in all my born days . . .
Actor 2	No, I've never either . . . but the preacher said I was truly special . . . a picture, she said.
Actor 1	A picture? How could she be so blind? I mean, a van Gogh, that's a picture, a Renoir, a Gainsborough . . . but you? You're a weed, for goodness' sake!
Actor 2	Yes, well, the preacher said I was a picture of faith. A faith that's tough and doesn't give up, a faith that's hardy and grows in the most difficult places, a faith that's ordinary and everyday and gets everywhere. A faith that can't be destroyed but has deep roots that are impossible to destroy. She said, if only every Christian could have a faith like mine rather than . . .
Actor 1	Rather than what? Come, come, I demand to know!
Actor 2	Rather than being an over-dramatic, here-one-day-gone-the-next, self-important glory seeker like some dahlias.
Actor 1	I . . . I . . . this is outrageous! For once I'm lost for words! How could they? I am a dahlia! That's a very important flower you know. This is not the end of this little event, you know . . . oh no, I'm off to a higher authority. Self-important? Moi? I'm off to find Alan Titchmarsh. *(Stalks off)*
Actor 2	So, the question is . . . what kind of faith do you have? Oh, and sorry about my seeds. I know . . . they spread everywhere, don't they?

Harvest 2

Seeds   *Genesis 8.15–22*
This simple two-narrator piece needs to be delivered slickly. A seed and a flower-pot are needed. No special costuming is necessary.

One	You never know, do you?
Two	*(Entering)* Know what?
One	How it's all going to work out.

Two	How what is going to work out?
One	You never know where it's going to go – what it's going to do.
Two	Will you stop talking in riddles just for one second?
One	Okay. *(Holds up a seed)* What is this?
Two	It looks like a seed.
One	You're absolutely right. And what will happen if I plant this in the ground and water it?
Two	*(Impatient at being treated like a child)* Are you really asking me this?
One	Be patient – we're getting there.
Two	Okay – I'll play along. Assuming you have prepared the ground properly, it will grow.
One	Brilliant. But what we don't know is how it will grow.
Two	What do you mean?
One	Well – the plant that grows from this seed – even if you know what kind of seed this is, you don't know how it will grow. It could be a great big plant.
Two	Or really tiny.
One	It could produce loads of tasty fruit.
Two	Or get hit by a frost on the first day of blossom.
One	It could help to provide a family with a living.
Two	And what about the seeds that this seed will produce?
One	Oooh – that's a bit mind-blowing. In this seed are the potential for whole forests of trees, fields full of vegetables. Orchard upon orchard of apples, year after year after year.
Two	All right, calm down.
One	But don't you see? Whole towns could be fed. Hundreds – thousands – of people's lives could be affected. All because of this one tiny, insignificant seed. *(Holds up seed)* Just look at it.
Two	I have to admit that it's all pretty amazing. People's lives around the world transformed by one little seed. Although . . . none of that is going to happen.
One	Why on earth not?
Two	You – clever clogs – have forgotten one small but vital fact.
One	And what, pray tell, is that?
Two	In order for lives to be given hope and the world to change and all that other good stuff . . .
One	*(Impatient)* Yes?
Two	*(Producing flowerpot)* You've got to plant it.

Harvest 3

Don't worry   *Matthew 6.25–33*

Carstairs, an elderly explorer, sits centrally, writing. Frobisher is eager and interested. Both are extremely posh! A chair, desk, pen and paper are needed. If they could be dressed in tweeds, it would add to the atmosphere.

Carstairs   'It was the dead of the African night. Coming from outside my tent, I could hear the cries of hungry wild animals surrounding me, moving in for the kill. I knew that my very life was in dire danger. I cast my eye around the bivouac to see whether there was any object in my possession that could aid me in my plight, and realized that I only possessed two old socks, a pencil sharpener and a mouldy bread roll.'

Enter Frobisher, who walks across to Carstairs, hand outstretched

Frobisher   Well, what ho, Carstairs, just up in the smoke for the day and knew that if I popped in on my old muckers at the Secret Daredevil Explorers and Silly Adventurers Club I'd come across you. Still slaving away at the old writing, eh?

Carstairs   Ah, Frobisher, devilishly good to see you. Just completing the sixteenth volume of the extraordinary adventures of my life. Going to call the latest chapter 'Saved by a mouldy bread roll in the jungle'.

Frobisher   Sounds top notch. If you don't mind my asking, what kind of bread roll was it?

Carstairs   I say Frobisher, what's that got to do with anything?

Frobisher   Well, nothing really – it just so happens that I am a bit of a bread fiend. Love the stuff – the smell of a freshly baked loaf is my idea of heaven. Delish! And anyway, it adds a nice dash of detail to the story . . . what!

Carstairs   You know, thinking of my adventurous times in Africa I can't help pondering how things are now.

Frobisher   Not enough food of any kind to go around these days – let alone bread.

Carstairs   Indeed not. I sit in church on Sundays and listen to the sermons of my favourite adventurous vicar, the Revd Samuel Peabody-Smyth. He says that Jesus talked about being bread, you know.

Frobisher   Did he? Gracious me.

Carstairs	Yes . . . living bread – dashed if I understand it.
Frobisher	Well, being the Son of the Almighty, and all that, I'm sure that he knew what he was talking about.
Carstairs	Yes – well, I'm pretty sure it's got nothing to do with my showing Christian kindness in my life.
Frobisher	Oh, absolutely not. The next thing you'll be thinking is that we've got a responsibility to help people who are starving to death. I can't imagine 'living bread' means that.
Carstairs	No. The idea of spiritual fruit being seen in your life? What tosh.
Frobisher	Quite right . . . give me a silly adventure in an exotic location any day.
Carstairs	Indeed – you know, it reminds me of the time when I was hanging by a vine, dangling over a ravine filled with alligators snapping their hungry jaws below me. I searched my pockets to discover that all I had was an old candle, three playing cards and a rusty nail.
Frobisher	You see – now who needs talk of living bread and spiritual commitments when you can have a very silly adventure instead? Tally ho!

11

Remembrance Sunday

Remembrance Sunday 1

Weep with those who weep   *Micah 4.1–8*
Two angels are looking downwards. They are heartbroken at what they see. No special costuming is necessary.

Michael	Look at them down there Gabriel.
Gabriel	I'm afraid I can hardly bring myself to look, Michael.
Michael	I know what you mean. I can't think what gets into their heads.
Gabriel	War, fighting, violence everywhere.
Michael	The things that we see every day – you'd think that as angels, there would be something we could do.
Gabriel	You know we're not allowed.
Michael	But how can God bear it?
Gabriel	He can't, he weeps every day as we do.
Michael	I saw a terrorist attack on a school bus yesterday – almost an entire group of schoolgirls wiped out, only one survivor.
Gabriel	What gets into their heads? What do they think they're going to achieve? What is going on in the mind of a person who can do that?
Michael	Do they have any sense at all of the pain and heartache they cause?
Gabriel	They can't do. Because if they'd seen the mothers' tears as we have, the broken hearts . . .
Michael	Then they wouldn't do it.
Gabriel	Exactly. How many wars have we seen, Michael?
Michael	I dread to think. I've watched torture, bloodshed, and people dying in the most horrible ways imaginable, innocent people caught up in the conflicts.
Gabriel	And what's it about? Power, land, politics . . .
Michael	And heaven help us . . . religion.
Gabriel	How dare they?

Michael	It's almost as if they'd never read the Bible.
Gabriel	Or the Koran, or any one of the sacred texts that they've got.
Michael	And, of course, the people who start the fighting . . .
Gabriel	Are always the ones farthest behind the front line.
Michael	You'd think that after all these years they'd be tired of it. That after all the appalling examples they'd have realized by now that the only thing that results from war is misery.
Gabriel	But instead of that they just pour money and resources into inventing new and ever more efficient and deadly ways of killing each other.
Michael	All of that God-given creativity and imagination squandered . . .
Gabriel	What a heartbreaking waste.
Michael	It's a scandal. That's what it is. How could they?
Gabriel	Didn't we tell them that Jesus was the Prince of Peace?
Michael	I distinctly remember taking the choir down there and singing about it.
Gabriel	Oh, that was a lovely night.
Michael	Sheep, shepherds, shocked expressions . . . it was great.
Gabriel	They wrote it down too.
Michael	In the Bible . . . I remember.
Gabriel	And it's not like most of them haven't got a copy of that on their bookshelf at home.
Michael	Some of them even read it.
Gabriel	So why don't they take notice of what it says then?
Michael	Who knows? It's almost as if they enjoy hating each other . . .
Gabriel	And fighting.
Michael	Lives shattered.
Gabriel	Bodies broken.
Michael	While we sit.
Gabriel	And watch.
Michael	And weep with those who weep.
Gabriel	And stir the hearts of those who work for peace.

Remembrance Sunday 2

Rosie and Jack   *Matthew 5.1–12*

*Two actors – one male, one female. Rosie sits to one side, Jack stands separately.
They are telling parts of the same story from different perspectives. Rosie is a*

boarding-house matron from a school in 1914. Jack is one of her pupils. Costumes are not strictly necessary but would add to the impact.

Jack	And I heard the sound of crows squawking in the morning mist . . .
Rosie	*(Speaking to the audience)* I had such fond memories of all of them – they were *my* boys, you see. I can hardly believe it.
Jack	And the crack of shells shattered the peace . . .
Rosie	I was so proud of them. I know it's silly. But I was like their mother, wasn't I? Well, it stands to reason, doesn't it? A boarding school – them spending most of their lives here. They saw more of me than their mums and dads.
Jack	And the splatter of mud as it flew through the air . . .
Rosie	And they've gone on to great things, some of my boys. Engineers and doctors, businessmen and lawyers . . . great things. And then the war came.
Jack	The sound of whimpers and screams cutting through the mist . . .
Rosie	And they were so keen to join up, most of them. 'To serve King and Country; that must be the greatest honour of all,' they'd say. I'd say, 'It's 1914, we're in the modern world now – that just means they're always coming up with new and better ways to kill young lads.' And they'd say, 'Oh matron, don't be so daft, we'll be home for Christmas' . . . I knew they wouldn't be.
Jack	The shouts of men, clambering over the top . . .
Rosie	It was a glorious summer that year. June was wonderful, and on Wednesday afternoons they had sport, and I'd sneak out and watch them playing cricket in a blaze of summer sunshine. They looked wonderful in their cricketing whites, not a care in the world, celebrating life. It was good to be alive and watching them. All of that goodness, all of that joy and potential and wonder. They'd come in for tea and scoff platefuls of sandwiches and drink lemonade. Seventeen years old they were – the whole of life stretching out before them.
Jack	The squelch of boots sinking into wet mud . . .
Rosie	And as I sat there on that glorious afternoon watching them in the summer haze, laughing and joking and enjoying life, I suddenly felt cold, and a shiver ran down my back.
Jack	We were frightened, you see, and young, so young.

Rosie	Jack Rutherford went out in August. I'd watched him play cricket a month before, and by September he was at the front line stuck in some godforsaken trench somewhere I'd never heard of. And that's where he died. It was October. They brought his body back, and we buried him in the graveyard. He wasn't the first, and he wasn't going to be the last. But he was one of my boys, and that . . . well, it meant something. I'll never forget the look on his mother's face at the funeral. Frightening, like all the life had been drained out of her. I couldn't believe it. I'd watched him play cricket just three months before. He had so much to offer, so much in front of him waiting to be grasped. And now he's dead.
Jack	I didn't want to die.
Rosie	And I wonder what God must make of all this. Such senseless waste, such cruel loss. No reason, no point . . . just death. I can't help but believe that God cries along with us. He must think we're mad.
Jack	And I heard the sound of the crows squawking in the morning mist.

Remembrance Sunday 3

The museum   *Matthew 5.43–8*

The curator and visitor enter – obviously on a guided tour. A brief sentence of introduction might help to root the action immediately. No special costuming is necessary.

Curator	Welcome, everybody, welcome. Come in to the Museum of Human Frailty. In this collection we have brought together artefacts that show how silly, vain, greedy and violent human beings can be.
Visitor	It sounds fascinating.
Curator	Madam, you have no idea. Here we have a genuine diamond-encrusted designer necklace worn by an actress to a ceremony called the 'Oscars' in 2002. It cost £4 million. The very next day the very same actress made a statement about how important the issue of world poverty was to her.
Visitor	I can hardly believe it.
Curator	I know, I know. From where we stand in the twenty-second century it does sound rather bizarre. But I have to say that the

	most important part of our display here in the museum is our War Room.
Visitor	Oh, of course, they still went to war with each other, didn't they?
Curator	Oh yes. World peace was only a distant dream, hoped for and prayed for by a group of brave and courageous individuals. This was an age of fear and hatred, of landmines and anthrax threats, of wars against terror and a massive arms trade, of children with guns and terrible acts of destruction.
Visitor	I can hardly imagine it.
Curator	I know . . . it's difficult. We have in our collection the most horrific selection of devices used to inflict unimaginable pain and suffering, damaging life in every way possible. And, unfortunately, we also have photos to prove they were used.
Visitor	And yet throughout this terrible period I've read that there were people who never lost hope. People in large numbers who continued to remember the sacrifice of those who had died and worked and prayed for peace.
Curator	Indeed, and as we now know, their prayers and actions were crucial to the progress that eventually took place.
Visitor	It's just as well they didn't give up.
Curator	Even though they must have wondered whether they were making any headway at all sometimes. I really recommend you have a look at our audio and visual archive, where we have thousands of entries from ordinary people testifying to how important remembrance was on the way to discovering peace. It really is very moving.
Visitor	I'll be sure to have a close look. This certainly sounds like a fascinating collection.
Curator	It is remarkable. And it's absolutely vital that we don't let memories like this fade away. We really must remember what humans are capable of doing to each other – the horror and the human sacrifice of war. And we need to remember how important continued prayer is. Do continue your visit – hear the stories that are to be told. It's in remembering that we protect the future.
Visitor	Thank you. Thank you very much.

They exit.

12

Creative Writing for Worship

Alan Ayckbourn, the well-known playwright, in his wonderful book *The Crafty Art of Playmaking*, says this in the introduction: 'I'm rarely one to theorize and when I try, I tend to get myself in the most awful tangle and have doubtless confused many more would-be authors . . . than I've ever managed to help.' Not that I'm comparing myself with Alan Ayckbourn, but in this case I know how he feels.

Why drama?

Life is essentially dramatic. Small-scale dramas happen all the time. I have a very vivid memory of standing in a Post Office in the build-up to Christmas one year. The man in front of me in the queue was actually returning some Christmas stamps that he had bought at that Post Office the day before. They were second-class Christmas stamps, and they had an artist's interpretation of Jesus on them. The man was in a state of some upset and wanted to exchange these pictorial stamps for a normal everyday set of stamps with the Queen's head on them. It wasn't that he objected to religious images being used on stamps in general, but he did object strongly to this particular picture of Jesus. 'That's not the picture of Jesus I was given in Sunday School,' he said in a loud voice. And carried on to explain that there was no way in which he would feel comfortable attaching that particular artist's rendering of the Christ-child on his Christmas cards and letters. I stood transfixed. What should I do? I was wearing nothing that identified me as a minister of religion. Should I reveal who I was and try and talk to the man about images of Jesus? Should I use the opportunity to talk about faith? Should I keep quiet and hope against hope that nobody in the Post Office recognized me? You see what I mean? Life is essentially dramatic. Small-scale dramas take place all around us every day. And worship itself is a piece of drama in all kinds of ways.

Creative writing

While there are many fine examples of collaboration in writing (look no further than the King James Bible), for me and for many others, writing is essentially a lone task. There you are, at a computer keyboard, waiting for inspiration to strike or words to come. If they don't, you go and make a cup of tea, pace around the house a bit and hopefully something will begin to make its way up from somewhere in the bottom of your mind to a place where you can get access to it and put it on paper. Discovering what you can do to help that to happen is a deeply personal process and will be different for everyone.

However, it might be worth having a discussion about some of the peculiarities of creative writing for the worship environment and sharing some things that I keep in mind when putting thoughts on paper. Part of the reason for doing this is to encourage you in your own attempts at creative writing. There are plenty of examples here to use, and do feel free to chop up and change the pieces that are in this book to suit your own environment. And that is an important part of this process because only you know the church, house group, school assembly or other gathering that you are going to be working with. You know their ages, how many of them there are, what their experience is. You are the one who has a voice that they might listen to and learn from. You are the one who knows what has gone down well, what they have responded to in the past or might find of interest in the future. Please do find within these pages an encouragement to do some creative writing of your own. Work up some ideas, knock them around a bit, perhaps try them out in small ways at first. As you get more experience and confidence, who knows what might happen?

Creative writing that is specifically meant to be read out loud in front of groups of people is a particular task. Think about the words you are using and how they are strung together. Try reading them out loud at home. How do they sound? Do they hang together well? Do the pauses work? Is the train of thought easy to follow in a situation where people can't go back to the beginning of the paragraph and check the meaning? All of these are vital questions that you need to ask yourself again and again as you continue to write.

If it's a monologue, does the character of the individual come through? Does he or she have a distinctive voice? Can you imagine that person sitting in front of you saying those words? Do some of the thoughts sound a little forced? Have you tried too hard to get the meaning that you want to convey across at the expense of the character? If the character holds true then the meaning should come through naturally. If it's a meditation, have you been honest with the feelings? One of the things that strikes me again and again about the Psalms is their brutal, painful, fantastic honesty. God is criticized, screamed at, questioned, praised, laughed with. If you are honest about how you have found the journey of faith or you are truthful about your understanding of the verses you are looking at, then others will respond to that honesty that they see in you even if they haven't had those feelings themselves. If the writing is a piece of drama, a sketch perhaps, is it engaging? Does it hold the attention? Sketches often use caricatures of people because there isn't time in a three or four minute piece to do an in-depth character study. Do those caricatures work? Does the point come across? Let's be honest about this right at the start. If you're doing a piece of creative writing for worship, there is some meaning you want to convey, some underlying understanding of faith and God and the human condition that you want to get across. Is that happening?

The place within worship

Let us assume for a moment that you are using one of the pieces in this book or that you are doing some creative writing of your own for worship (clearly there are other events where this kind of writing could be used – house groups, school assemblies and so on).

There are a number of questions that you need to ask yourself. How long is the piece to be? A piece of creative writing could take the place of the sermon slot entirely. It could be a story or parable in place of the address. In which case, a great deal of thought needs to be put into it. What is the main theme of the service? How is this piece of writing best going to serve the theme? How many people are going to be needed to perform it? Have you got the right people in the congregation to help? A long piece of creative writing delivered by a group of people will take some time to prepare and rehearse. Do you have that kind of time? Be aware of the limitations of the particular space and group of people that you are working with. That is not to say that you should never stretch yourself and others, but it would be wrong to ask a group to perform something they were clearly out of their depth with.

In most cases a piece of creative writing will be there to expand on or develop some thinking that will be taken up later in the worship. Make sure your piece does just that and does not exist as a sideline or, worse, a distraction from the main theme of the service. Work with the leader of the worship (if you are the leader so much the better). Know how the piece fits. Ask yourself how the congregation will react, and think about the space that you will perform/read in. Is there anything that you can do to get the message of the piece across by movement or emphasis? Are the congregation used to new things happening or will this come as a great shock and surprise?

The process

All I can really tell you is how the pieces in this book came to be. The way *you* do things may well be different. I start with the scripture reading first. I lay out all three readings (Old Testament, Gospel and Epistle) for the day, and I read them. I look for any connecting themes between the readings. Is there connective material that tells you why they were linked together on this particular lectionary Sunday? Consult commentaries. Your first response to a reading is important, and you need to hold on to that set of feelings that you had on the initial reading. However, you must try and avoid careless use of the material, and a good commentary will identify issues and help you to sort out any complicated ideas.

If the reading is recounting an event or telling a story, ask yourself who else might have been there. What were their thoughts (see the monologue by the honey seller talking about John the Baptist on pp. 12–13)? What happened before the story took place (see the dialogue between Zechariah and Elizabeth on pp. 37–9)? If you are looking at a parable, what are the thoughts of some of the characters involved? Is there an interesting and unusual way to get into the material? Asking questions of the text will give you routes into it and ideas that may form the basis for an exciting piece of imaginative writing. It also helps the congregation to enter into the biblical world. Seeing a well-known story through different eyes, being given permission to ask yourself 'what if' questions, is a vital creative tool.

In the case of prophecies or epistles, look for key words or phrases that leap out at you. What is the general feel of the piece? If it is an exciting, vibrant poem of praise, how do you convey that emotion in words? It is easy to think back to moments when we have felt an overwhelming sense of praise – it is more difficult to recreate that sense from biblical words that are often already well known. Sometimes people just need to be given some time to approach that feeling for themselves. I was surprised in the writing of this book how many times I was deeply moved by a piece of writing that I thought I knew well. Giving a piece time for its emotional intent to dawn on you is important. Do not rush into writing. Read the scripture and then go off and do something else for a while. Allow the thought and intention of the piece to sink in.

In writing meditations, try to be as honest, both to the thought-world of the biblical passage and to your own response to it. If the emotion is honest then people will respond.

I am completely committed to the idea of the use of creative writing within worship. It opens windows on biblical truth and experience, it helps people to understand the scriptures more fully, it makes people think and ask questions in ways they might not do in any other way. It might even occasionally bring a smile to people's faces, and that is never a bad thing. I wish you well as you use this material and as you explore creative writing for yourself.

Index of Bible Passages

Thematic Index